BEYOND HIS CONTROL

To Mary Helen, hope
you "enjoy" this book.
with love,
Linda

Linda Hale Bucklin

BEYOND HIS CONTROL

Memories of a Disobedient Daughter

Linda Hale Bucklin

Hope Publishing House
Pasadena, California

For information address:

Hope Publishing House
P.O. Box 60008
Pasadena, CA 91116 - U.S.A.
Tel: (626) 792-6123 / Fax: (626) 792-2121
E-mail: hopepub@sbcglobal.net
Web site: www.hope-pub.com

Printed on acid-free paper

Library of Congress Cataloging-in-Publication Data

Bucklin, Linda.
  Beyond his control : memories of a disobedient daughter / Linda Hale Bucklin ; foreword by Alan Jones.
    p. cm.
  ISBN 13: 978-1-932717-12-9 (trade pbk. : alk. paper)
  ISBN 10: 1-932717-12-9 (trade pbk. : alk. paper)
  1. Bucklin, Linda. 2. Problem families--California--Biography. 3. California--Biography. 4. Interpersonal Relations--California. I. Title.
CT275.B78473A3 2006
979.4'6053092--dc22
  [B]   2006102334

Contents

Dedicated

to my beloved mother

Marialice Patricia King Hale

1912-1969

Foreword

I found Linda Bucklin's book very moving and inspiring. She could have so easily made a gossipy self-justifying book, but she managed a near miracle in telling the truth with compassion and by being both honest and kind, utterly herself yet inclusive. I thought the last few pages particularly moving as she saw her father (and indeed all of us) as God sees us. It will be good news for all who read it.

She shares with us a hard yet tender story. We are all called to practice the art of living truthfully. It's the only way we can find our own true path. But how do we "declare" who we are without our testimony being at someone else's expense? The danger of a memoir is that we paint ourselves always in a good light. Our mistakes are forgivable and those of the ones who have hurt us are not. Linda Bucklin's fierce honesty avoids these traps, and we have a story to challenge and touch the heart—that of a daughter who stood up against her father and deeply loved him to the end. That's why this story is not only Linda's story. Its truth is universal.

Mary Oliver in her poem "The Journey" echoes Linda's truth:

One day you finally knew
what you had to do, and began,
though the voices around you
kept shouting
their bad advice – ...
But little by little,
as you left their voices behind,
the stars began to burn
through the sheets of clouds,
and there was a new voice,
which you slowly
recognized as your own,
that kept you company
as you strode deeper and deeper
into the world,
determined to do
the only thing you could do –
determined to save
the only life you could save.

The paradox of love is that the work of "saving one's own soul" is not a selfish and egotistical act. It is a work which serves and heals us all. "In the end," writes St. John of the Cross, "we shall be examined in love." This book bears witness to that and will be good news for all who read it.

– *The Very Reverend Alan Jones, Ph.D., OBE, Dean, Grace Cathedral, San Francisco is author of many books on spiritual life.*

Acknowledgements

I could not have written this book without the help and encouragement of many people, angels in my life, who with their love and wisdom have guided, inspired and supported me throughout this long journey.

In chronological order, I'd like to thank those friends who read early drafts and cheered me on: Kathleen Sullivan Alioto, Mary Keil, Myron Wick, Dr. John Bockstoce, Allan Stone, Barbara Goldie, Hilary Spencer, Hap Hale, Anne Pattee, Connie Price, Mimi and Ron Reich, Dick Carlson and Charlie Hoeveler.

Special thanks to Dr. Steven Newmark who helped me find and follow my north star. I am grateful to my legal angels, Peter Folger, Thomas Burke, Dom Campisi, and Nancy Levin, for their wise counsel. Many thanks also to Diana Scott, Caroline Pincus, and Thea Sullivan for their brilliant editorial skills and feedback, and also for their constant encouragement.

Thanks to my friend and former agent Brenda Feigen for believing strongly that I had a story to share. Thanks to Faith Annette Sand of Hope Publishing, who also believed.

I especially thank Dean Alan Jones, a mentor, for his friendship and inspiration.

I must thank my three wonderful sons, Christian, John and Nick, for their understanding and love, and also my lovely daughter-in-law Kris for her insights and enthusiasm.

I am forever grateful to my dear husband Bill who has never stopped being my champion. I thank him for his reading and rereading every draft, for his belief in the power of my story and in me. With his love and unwavering support, he helped me find my way.

Dare to declare who you are.
It is not far from the shores of silence
to the boundaries of speech.
The road is not long
but the way is deep.
And you must not only walk there,
you must be prepared to leap.
—Hildegard of Bingen

Introduction

The phone rang at 9:40 P.M., March 25, 1969. I heard my father's voice at the other end of the line. "I think your mother's hurt herself," he said. "You and J.B. better come over right away." My husband of two months and I quickly dressed and drove over to 2920 Broadway Street, to the house I lived in until I was married. When we arrived, Dad was downstairs watching television in the library, a small room off to the right of the massive front door. Walking slowly, he led us down the long hall and up the curving staircase to the second floor. He motioned towards his study, which was adjacent to my parents' bedroom.

As I moved towards the door, my new husband stopped me. "Wait," he said. "I'll go." Ashen faced, he returned to my side. "Your mother hasn't injured herself; she's dead." He called 911. Minutes later the normally quiet block was invaded by flashing red lights, policemen and a few reporters who materialized out of the dark. I couldn't bring myself to go into the room where she was. Only my imagination and a description I later read in the coroner's report painted a picture of how she must have looked. Off in the corner near the closet where my father's suits hung, she was lying motionless, her slim, white legs tangled in the folds of her silk nightgown, her right temple blown apart by the force of a .38 caliber bullet from my father's pistol.

My younger brother, home on vacation from boarding school and ready to spread his wings at Stanford, was out with friends. I worried about what he'd think when he saw all the police cars in front of our house, so we waited for him outside. When he finally arrived, J.B. and I told him Mom was dead. Before I could register his response, Dick Miller, Police Commissioner and a good friend of my parents, bustled in, still dressed in his white tie and tails, having left Symphony Hall to rush to our home.

At different times, both he and my father had served as President of the San Francisco Opera Association. More than that connection, however, they belonged to the old boys' network, that elite world of the Bohemian Grove, Pacific Union Club, Burlingame Country Club. They were "to the manor born," members of a fraternity where loyalty ran deep and image and keeping up appearances mattered above all else. Mr. Miller took over, talking to the officers in charge. Soon thereafter, the homicide team was dismissed.

Later, a good friend of mine, an investigative reporter, told me he'd heard on his radio that night that there'd been a shooting on outer Broadway Street and headed to our house. When he arrived, he wasn't allowed in, but he talked to the San Francisco police officers who were there. Suspicious of my father's initial behavior of distancing himself from the scene, they were upset that Homicide was so quickly called off the case. They had never seen a man whose wife had just committed suicide display so little emotion, they told my friend. And when they later questioned my father in his study, they were shocked that he had no compunction whatsoever about readily approaching the body, stepping back and forth over his dead wife's head as if she were a rock he didn't want to trip on.

And then Marion, one of Mom's best friends from Los Angeles, called me in tears, unwilling to believe the news that my mother had killed herself. Hours before my mother died, they'd had a long telephone conversation during which my mother apparently had rehashed many details of my father's involvement with Denise Minnelli, then-wife of Hollywood director Vincente Minnelli. Only recently had my parents had any real connection with the Hollywood set and my mother had confided in Marion that she felt it was an odd match socially. My parents were from the staid, conservative world of old San Francisco, with little in common with the trendy Hollywood social scene.

My mother had heard of Denise's reputation as a gifted hostess who was reputed to have an unerring ability to gather together interesting, talented people. She was the one who dictated who was in (and included in her parties) and who was out (and excluded), effectively controlling those people who feared being socially ostracized. My mother had also, apparently, heard much speculation about Denise's climb to power.

That night my mother also had told Marion about the invitation she'd opened addressed to Mr. and Mrs. Prentis Cobb Hale from Mr. and Mrs. Jules Stein, two of the most powerful people in Hollywood. Mentioning it to Dad, she had said, "Prentis, this might be fun," and he had replied, "Yes, it will be, but you're not invited."

She had been terribly hurt by his response, she'd told Marion, especially when she'd later discovered that my father had been seated next to Denise at the party. Decades later I read an October 2003 *HELLO!* article where Denise recounted that their attraction was immediate.

During this phone conversation, my mother had also remembered with some anguish how my father had insisted they invite the Minnellis to a dinner party they had hosted five months earlier before the opening of the opera in San Francisco. My mother told Marion that she had agreed to his demand, still pretending not to know what was going on.

Denise had showed up without her husband. As Marion retold the story to me, I actually remembered this party well. Dad had commanded me to be there for cocktails. Playing dumb as my mother did, I had stood in front of our beautiful painting by Berthe Morisot, the very painting over which Denise and my family would ultimately fight so publicly. I remember chatting nonchalantly with some of my parents' friends, all the while wondering what they thought of Denise being there.

I can still remember my father introducing me to Denise that night. She appeared to be years younger than he was and I was immediately struck by how confident and outgoing she seemed. She was wearing a strapless evening dress that showed off her smooth, white skin and her fawn-colored hair flipped upwards off her bare shoulders. We talked briefly, but I could hardly understand her because of her thick Serbian accent. Then Dad moved her on to meet more of the guests. Fortunately, I was not required to stay for dinner. Later, Renée, our French maid, had whispered to me that my mother had seated Denise in the place of honor, on Dad's right.

According to Marion, my mother hadn't wanted to believe that her husband might be attracted to Denise and had hoped he would come to his senses. Sure that this infatuation would pass, she had decided to wait patiently and avoid any confrontation, ignoring for the moment the storm that was gathering force within their marriage. But on the eve of her death in this final call, my mother had told Marion she'd accepted the ending of her 33-year marriage and was prepared to give Dad a divorce.

Hearing all this, I was without answers or words. Here she had told her best friend that she was prepared to agree to a divorce and now she was dead. After bowing to my father's will for so many years, did my mother feel that life without him was no longer worth living? Weren't her many friends, her four children and two grandchildren on the way reasons enough to bring joy back into her world?

I tried to piece together what might have happened that last night of my mother's life, to make sense of her thoughts and feelings those last few hours. After she had ended her telephone conversation, did she sit there at her desk and look out her bedroom window at the sunset painting the sky beyond the Golden Gate Bridge?

Knowing that her husband no longer loved her, did she go through the motions of having a civilized dinner with him, or did she take to her bed, her brown Burmese cat, Cocie, nestled in her lap, preferring books to strained conversation? Did she and my father have words, words that made up her undecided mind? Or had she already decided to take her own life?

Questions I couldn't answer tumbled through my mind. Was she alone when she died or had my father been there?

If they were together, did she make a final plea to him and then threaten to kill herself? "Prentis, you are the man I've always loved and you know that I've always done everything in my power to please you. My heart is breaking; how can you be with that woman? I can't live with the pain of your not loving me anymore; I am going to shoot myself."

Did she hope these words would shock him into loving her again? Did he call her bluff or was he silent? Did she decide on her own to take his gun from his top drawer or did he dare her to?

I couldn't bear to imagine my mother alone, distraught, feeling she no longer had any reason to live, putting Dad's pistol to her head and pulling the trigger. It was just as devastating to imagine my father, nearby or even by her side, detached, perhaps even saying the very words he knew would put her over the edge. Did she act from an angry place or one of deep despair? Any scenario was too terrible to consider; I closed my eyes, no longer allowing my imagination to touch any corner of my mother's death.

A few days later we drove to Halstead's Funeral Home for the wake. She lay in an open coffin. Her lips were red, her hair was perfectly combed with one wave brushing across her forehead – she looked as if she had just stepped out of the beauty parlor. I even saw the brown beauty mark she always painted high on her cheek. She was wearing her new yellow wool suit and there perched on the collar was the gold and blue enamel hummingbird pin she loved. As she lay there so still and unmoving, all dressed up for an opera meeting or luncheon party, I couldn't grasp that she was really dead. Any moment I expected her to open her eyes, sit up and say, "Goodness, gracious, what am I doing here taking it so easy?"

Motionless, I stood there by her side until Dad pushed me forward. I watched as he stepped up to the casket. Putting on his glasses, he leaned over and peered down into the silk padded interior. After he inspected her for many long minutes, he said to no one in particular, "My, they certainly did a good job; you'd never know." I wanted to hit him. I was furious that even with this tragedy, what was most important to him was how well my mother looked in death. But as usual I couldn't speak.

When my father later announced that we were never to talk of my mother's suicide, I was secretly relieved. I followed his dictates, afraid of him and not courageous enough to disobey. But no matter how hard I tried to suppress any thoughts of my mother, she was never far from my conscious thought.

Soon after the funeral, my father and Denise took off for Europe and I began my life as a newlywed. True to form as a representative of the Hale family, I acted as if nothing had happened. I went through the motions of being an enthusiastic new bride. My husband and I entertained, went on ski trips, fished small streams in northern California and spent many weekends at my family's beloved ranch. It was there that I felt most grounded, most at home in my heart.

On one such weekend, just four months after my mother's death, we hosted a house party there. It was July, 1969, and ten of us were sitting on the porch, laughing and drinking Mai Tais and waiting for the full moon to rise. When it was high in the night sky, we jostled our way into my parents' bedroom and turned on their tiny, black and white T.V. There on the fuzzy screen we watched Neil Armstrong take his first step on the moon.

I was perched on my mother's side of the bed. Whether it was the excitement of that moment or the spell of alcohol, or both, I will never know, but I could feel my mother behind me. Thinking I was blocking her view and not wanting her to miss a moment of this historic event, I moved over and patted a place for her to sit next to me. But when I turned around, there was no one there. I gulped down my drink and ran outside with the others to cheer and dance under the light of the moon.

In the years that followed, my brothers, my sister and I continued living our lives, but nothing was ever the same. No matter how hard we tried, we no longer fit together. I ultimately went into therapy to help me through my grief and guilt over my mother's death, but the psychiatrist I chose (recommended by my father's doctor) spent much of our sessions looking up names I mentioned in a copy of the Social Register he had on his desk. Even though I was hurting badly, I never felt safe enough to express my feelings to him.

After he sent me to a specialist who gave me the Rorschach test, he read me parts of this confidential report about me. "Mrs. M. is not a particularly insightful person nor is she prepared to go very far beyond the surface of the events of her life. I would expect that dealing with her could be fairly laborious. She handled the test in a superficial and fragmented manner."

Hurt and upset, I ended my sessions. Even so, I suspected there was much truth to these words and found another psychiatrist, one whom I learned to trust. Five years later, I walked away from my marriage. Difficult as it was to leave a fine husband and loving, supportive in laws who had provided the family I craved, I knew the marriage had never been right for J.B. and me. This was the first step I had ever taken for myself.

Even though at that time I appeared extroverted and confident, inside I was full of questions about who I was, what I thought, what I wanted, what I deserved. As a child I had been very shy, reluctant even to read aloud in class. My father had put me in constant fear of being wrong or making a mistake. I was used to my father telling me how to think, how not to feel and how to do only what he wanted. When it came to living life, I was ambivalent and inexperienced. But now I could no longer ignore the yearning to express myself and hear my own voice.

After the divorce, I began to take tiny steps to express myself in the world. Always interested in people and their stories, I was hired to write profiles of interesting people for a small, local newspaper and then for the *Journal of Commerce,* a daily newspaper in New York. Every time an article appeared, I felt excited and then afraid that I was upsetting my father by having my words printed for many people to read.

Even when I had an article published in a national magazine, my father gave me little credit. Putting on his glasses, he flipped through the pages, commenting only on the beauty of the photographs, which had nothing to do with my contribution. He seemed unable to tolerate my achievement, as if doing so would weaken him in some way. Through writing these stories, however, I was slowly finding my way to my own.

During this time Alan Jones, dean of San Francisco's Grace Cathedral and also a friend, called to ask me to read a lesson at the Christmas Eve service. My throat immediately tightened. I couldn't say a word. But after a long silence I agreed to do so. When we hung up, I cried. Touched that I had a friend who wanted to celebrate me, I was at the same time still terrified that I would be unable to stand up and speak in front of so many people. But I decided that I must do it, for myself and for my mother.

When I walked down the aisle, I carried one of her handkerchiefs in my pocket. Standing at the lectern and looking out over everyone, I felt faint. But when I began to read the story of the Annunciation, I heard my voice, steady and resonant, spread across the huge cathedral and I forgot my fears. Instead I imagined my mother was listening proudly, happy to have a daughter who was brave enough to speak.

A heavy silence surrounding my mother's death persisted over the next few years. Even as I couldn't speak of her within our family, I kept her memory alive by staying in touch with her friends. They balanced me, lightening the stigma of her death by reminding me of how beloved she had been.

One Christmas, Mrs. Metcalf, a close friend, gave me two beautiful crystal wine glasses with the following note attached: "These glasses are the ones your mother gave us years ago to start a collection, which she added to every year. They have always been one of our dearest treasures and we are starting to return them to where they really belong. I know you will think of your fabulous, gentle, loving mother and all the joy she added to so many lives when you drink out of these. Your mother, my friend, was made of angels' wings. Pat was everybody's favorite. Here she was, the most meaningful part of your father and he just flew past her without looking. It was as if she didn't exist for him anymore. I think she was broken hearted as much for him as for herself."

Two years after my mother's death, my father married Denise Minnelli. I never really got to know Denise. We had occasional birthday lunches and some dinners and we exchanged Christmas presents. But that was about all. She seemed to like his money, power and social position and so did he.

With Denise by his side, my father began to shed all remnants of the family man he once claimed to be. The second Christmas after Mom's death, he and Denise went to our ranch with my younger brother, Hap. He told me it took Denise two days to open her mountain of presents. That same year, my husband and I celebrated Christmas in San Francisco. Traditionally, Dad would give me a lovely piece of jewelry and so I saved their present for last. Holding the oblong box, I shook it. The contents rattled, confirming my hunch it was something special. Excitedly I opened it, only to find two bars of soap in a box meant for three. On the bottom of the box was a sticker – "not for resale" and I realized that this was something Denise had gotten for free. I threw the box across the room.

Over the years that followed, my father made increasingly reckless and vengeful personal and financial decisions that adversely affected his children. By now I was in my early 30's and still trying to keep balanced in a world that had been turned upside down. And I was filled with questions for which I had no answers and not enough courage to face.

What really did occur the night my mother died? How could this have happened to a family like the Hales, one that from all appearances (and from my perspective as well) seemed so happy and successful? Would we weather this tragedy and go forward together in this life? Even if my mother hadn't, would I be able to withstand my father's force and find my way?

When my mother died, although my father never knew it, he lost the lifeline to his heart. But for me her death provided an unexpected opening, helping me lay claim to my life. Now I was determined to discover who I was and how I wanted to live what had been up to then an unexamined life. After so many years without hearing my own words, in the final silence of my mother's life, I began to speak.

1

Frances

In 1947 when I was two, we moved to 2920 Broadway Street, a large brick house on the westernmost block of Broadway. It was a magnificent building with panoramic views of the San Francisco Bay, Golden Gate Bridge and Marin hills beyond. When my father sold it in 1975 to Ingrid and Ruben Hills of Hills Bros. coffee, I remembered hearing they had a priest come to bless this home and chase away whatever demons might still be lingering in the hallways.

But for me these early years were happy ones. Aside from my parents, my sister Hilary, who was six and my brother Rusty, who was five, our entourage included Baba, the Japanese cook; Frances, my beloved nurse; Gee, a quiet Chinese man who was Dad's personal valet and house boy of all trades; Sugi, the Japanese laundress; Sinka, our Siamese cat; and Zibelene, Mom's black standard poodle.

We grew up in a world of privilege, on the one hand a

world of myriad opportunities and on the other, one of rules, expectations and punishments. There were good times when our family hung together tightly, when we laughed and enjoyed each other, when my mother played the piano and my father was kind. And there were also sad times when Dad's willful temper erupted, dampening our spirits and darkening our lives. We, the four children, tread water, trapped in the emotional eddy that encircled us. Even though we yearned to move beyond the deep-cut banks of my father's control into the larger currents of life, we didn't feel confident enough to venture far from home.

My parents viewed power through completely different lenses. Raised in a world of music and books, my mother drew strength from her creative and intellectual talents. With her many friends, she indulged in lively literary discussions. She also played the piano, frequented the symphony, ballet and opera. She cared little about money and social prestige; what mattered most to her was the world of ideas and the heart. She placed her faith in the power of love.

My father, the scion of a wealthy, prestigious San Francisco family, came from a world where money and societal power were of utmost importance. When my parents attended the opera, my mother was transported by the music, while my father was more interested in seeing who else important was there. He liked to be seen. Unlike my inward-looking mother, my father needed validation from the outside world, defining himself by how many boards he served on and how much money he made. His self-esteem was dependent on how rich and successful he became.

Like my mother I loved to read. One day Mother brought me home *A Little Princess*. Handing me the gilt-edged book, she said, "I hope you like this. The saleslady at Paul Elder's said it was perfect for a girl your age." It felt heavy and important, but I was worried I wouldn't like reading about princesses. Once into it, however, I became Sara, born into a wealthy family in India and then transplanted to England when both her parents died, with few possessions to her name. I couldn't put it down and cried throughout the story.

Like my father I was interested in the stock market page. Choosing a few stocks like Union Oil and Bank of America that I'd heard him mention, I'd follow them and chart their progress. Then I'd report back to my father whether or not I thought they might be a good investment. I felt grown-up and businesslike and knew I was pleasing my father by showing interest in money. As an adult I had difficulty integrating their two worlds, walking in both yet wondering where I really belonged. Whose world would I choose for my yardstick for happiness?

The first six years of my life revolved around my nurse, Frances. Unless I was at the ranch or on the beach at Aptos, I was always with her at 2920 Broadway Street; we were an inseparable duo, an island apart from the comings and goings of my parents and older siblings. When the rest of the family went to Palm Springs for a vacation, I happily stayed with Frances or visited her sister with her. Since I was too young to sit at the dinner table with the rest of the family, I ate in the kitchen with Frances, Baba and Gee.

Until I started kindergarten when I was only four years and four months old, I have few memories without Frances in them. I believe it was her healthy parenting that gave me the solid emotional foundation that sustained me in later life, affording me the strength I would eventually need to question my father's abusive authority.

One day Frances gave me two young parakeets, one yellow and one blue, both of which I loved. Soon they were tame enough to sit on my shoulders or my head and they accompanied me wherever I went. Even when I danced to the music Frances played for me on the phonograph, they kept their balance and I could feel their tiny feet scratching my scalp.

Baba's warm kitchen where Gee and Baba sat, busily chopping vegetables or shelling peas, was one of my favorite spots. On seeing me, they would stop everything. One time Baba scooped me onto his lap and pulled from his pocket a small acorn ball he'd brought home from the ranch and began carving. Soon I saw an owl emerging from its smooth surface. Carefully, I traced the outlines with my chubby fingers. I remember eating thick slices of white bread, covered in butter and sugar, singing loud songs and tapping my feet – slap, slap – against the linoleum floor. Oh, how they laughed and hugged me.

Once, hearing a rattle at the back door, I rushed to find the milkman, dropping off six glass bottles set in a wire basket. Spying me, he invited me for a ride in his truck. Frances, nearby, agreed and I trotted behind him down the back alley where he lifted me up into his white Borden's truck. I hung on tightly until he stopped at the end of the block where the gates to the Presidio stood. Frances was there, waiting. Walking back, hand-in-hand with Frances, I saw Gee sweeping up the front walk and I ran towards him, his face one big smile as I approached.

At our place at the beach in Aptos, a few hours south of

San Francisco, I would spend hours with Frances and Baba, building sand castles and sometimes I sat quietly in the dark of Rusty's special tent, thrilled when he invited me in. It was there I got stung by a bee, the first time I remembered feeling sad and hurt. Frances wrapped my arm in one of her big red handkerchiefs, which I wore long after the pain was gone.

One summer I shared a room with Rusty during a naptime when he was really too old to take a nap. Quickly, I fell asleep, but he, of course, didn't. Bored, he began rolling up tiny bits of Silly Putty which he threw, one by one, into my crib, where they became trapped in my curly hair. Coming in to awaken me, Frances smoothed my bangs off my forehead. Feeling some lumps, she realized my hair was one big mass of tangles. Furious, she scolded Rusty and I cried, upset that he was in trouble.

Frances taught me to read – before my fourth birthday and so my parents decided to send me to kindergarten that fall of 1949. Until then, I'd had little interaction with my peers, spending most of my waking hours with Frances. That first day of school, I clung to her, not wanting her to abandon me. We walked over to the fish aquarium. For a second, I was distracted and when I turned around, she was gone. Tears streamed down my cheeks as I stood silently by the tank, watching all the other mothers say their good-byes and wishing Frances were still by my side.

Suddenly, someone touched my shoulder and a voice said "Hi, my name is Lea; what's yours?" That first day, I worried when I didn't know all the names of the colors the teachers showed us. Lea whispered the answers to me. Smarter and older than I, she requested that her cot be placed next to mine at naptime. From that moment on, throughout grade school, we were best friends. In fourth grade, I was stumped by the word "offspring." She told me the answer, but I thought it meant some kind of water system and didn't believe her.

No matter where I was, if Frances was there I felt protected, loved and guided. She was my guardian angel and with her I was secure and eager to learn; like a sponge I soaked up all the love and wisdom that surrounded me.

Before my sixth birthday, I noticed that Mom was growing a big tummy. I remember the day I understood that soon I would have a new baby sister or brother. My mother called me to her bedroom. "Linda, I have some exciting news for you. I'm going to have a baby." But because I lived on the periphery of our family life, this news occasioned little reaction.

Soon thereafter summer began and I, at age six, went away for the first time without Frances, across the Bay to Belvedere, with our friends, the Metcalfs. They owned a lovely, brown-shingled summer house overlooking Angel Island and the San Francisco Bay beyond and had three daughters—Katie, my sister's friend; Lizzie, two years older than I; and Mary, two years younger. Sandwiched between the two, I gravitated more to Lizzie.

We would run wild through the tiered garden, all of us hiding behind huge ferns and then darting off to pluck ripe raspberries that grew near the vegetable garden. We'd pull up small carrots and eat them, too. I spent much of my time trying to keep up with Lizzie, whether we played kick the can, capture the flag, or just hung out on the dock. One day we fished for perch and Lizzie showed me how to press their fat bellies and watch the babies pop out, tiny silver slivers that we slipped back into the water.

Of course I followed Lizzie everywhere, in awe of her age and independence. She was allowed to take out their putt-putt, powered by a small 25 horsepower engine, alone in the bay, but only if we wore life jackets and only if we stayed in the leeward side, not straying beyond the tip of Belvedere that touched the open bay. One day, windless and hot, Lizzie snaked the boat along until we could see the Golden Gate Bridge. Suddenly, the water became choppy and I got wet and started to cry. Irritated, Lizzie turned homeward and I felt like a baby.

Suddenly, I wanted to go home and be with Frances. Before I could gather up my courage to tell Mrs. Metcalf that I was homesick, she called me to the phone. It was my father. "Linda, you have a new baby brother."

"Oh," I said. "I wish it had been a girl." Then I asked, "Can I come home? I want to come home and talk to Frances."

His voice tightened and he began to lecture me. "She's on vacation; what a silly girl you are not to appreciate all the Metcalfs are doing for you. You don't know how lucky you are."

When I finally did go home, Mom was there with my new baby brother, Hamilton, called Hap, short for Happiness. I didn't know why, but I didn't feel very happy. Touching his soft, bare head, I asked my mother, "How can you tell he's a boy? He has no hair."

Mom didn't answer; finally she said. "Linda, of course you know." I laughed and said nothing, not wanting her to realize that I had no clue. Then an unfamiliar woman, in a starched white uniform, walked in. My mother introduced us. "Linda, this is Miss Cooke; she is here to care for your new baby brother."

"Where is Frances?" I asked anxiously, as I watched Miss Cooke carefully pick up Hap.

"There, there," my mother said, "Frances is on vacation. She'll be back soon." Somehow, I sensed she was not telling me the truth and I was uneasy, but I lived with her answer for many months before I finally gave up all hope of her return.

With Frances gone, it seemed as if most of the sound had been sucked out of my world. I no longer heard her calling out for me, or basked in her excited exclamations over how I tied my shoes or what new book I was able to read. Nor did I sit, enchanted, listening to records with her, singing along, getting up to dance and twirl around, keeping time to the sound of her hands clapping in delight. Now there was only the new governess' stern, English-accented voice, so foreign to my ear, piercing the cocoon of silence that had wrapped itself around me.

When I was at home, I spent most of my time in my room, standing by my window that overlooked the street. Counting the squares on the tidy sidewalk below, I followed the lines for as far as I could see. I was waiting, waiting for my beloved Frances to return. In my hand I held a tiny, grey fawn, the last gift she had given me. Maybe, I thought, if I squeezed it hard enough, she would return. I stood on one foot and counted to ten and then switched, back and forth, back and forth, fearing that if I broke my rhythm, it would be my fault if Frances never came back.

At six years of age, I was considered old enough to walk the three blocks home from school by myself, something I had been eager and proud to do when Frances was still with me. But her absence changed everything. Now I ran home crazily, bursting into the house, out of breath, hoping she might be there. Unable to hide my despair when I saw Miss Cooke, who was giving Hap his afternoon bottle, I would rush back to the top of the hill from whence I came. I would wait, watching to see if I could spot Frances, my loving, strong, no-nonsense, reading-to-me, tucking-me-in-at-night, hugging-me-tight nurse, walking up that steep hill back to me.

This after-school ritual, punctuated by my evening vigil at my window became part of my life for months. I remember the wind in my face drying my tears and I remember the one time when my heart started pounding so swiftly I thought I might lose my breath. From the top of the hill, I'd spotted a small, bustling dot in the distance I was certain was Frances, until the woman stopped to readjust her parcel and I saw her face.

One dull, foggy day when the eucalyptus trees were dripping with dew, I was in the park with Miss Cooke and Hap. No one else was there. I eyed the empty swings and suddenly I remembered how Frances pushed me high, so high that I thought I could touch the clouds in the sky. Then she would catch me when I came back down, hugging me, telling me she loved me best of all. Watching Miss Cooke lean over my baby brother, carefully tucking the blanket in under his feet, I remembered just how much I loved Frances and panicked.

Wildly, I ran back to 2920 Broadway Street. Crying, I found my mother, busy at her desk and told her how much I hated Miss Cooke. Between sobs I asked her when Frances would be coming back. "You're a big girl now, Linda," she said. "You're too big to have a nurse. Frances is taking care of another little girl who's younger, who needs her more." Her words tumbled around me like a roaring waterfall and I felt as if I were suspended in space, looking down at my six year old body, my skinned knees and tear-stained cheeks, at my dark bangs pressed awkwardly on my forehead. I could not speak.

Later, my mother and Miss Cooke came in "to mend a few fences." As soon as I saw them together, I started to worry. Assuring me I didn't mean what I'd said earlier about hating Miss Cooke, my mother asked me to apologize for running off. With Frances gone and my mother now an ally of her replacement, I lost hope. "I'm sorry," I whispered.

Smoothing her crisp uniform, Miss Cooke said, "You've no business leaving like that. In England this would never happen." Then my mother suggested I give Miss Cooke a hug. Not daring to disobey because I was now so worried my mother would leave me, too, I put my arms around Hap's nurse. I felt her padded corset and stiff spine, so different from the soft, rounded curves of Frances, and my sadness deepened.

Only Gee, my father's houseboy, noticed how sad I was. He couldn't speak English and I couldn't speak Chinese, but his eyes told me he knew of my pain and longing. I sought out his company as much as I could. Weekends, he made hats out of paper bags, one for him and one for me and I stood outside watching him sweep our steps. Comforted by his quiet presence, I followed him around as he watered the garden and searched in dark corners for the snapping turtle that lived there.

In an instant, my life had changed dramatically. Frances,

my protector, was no longer there and my place as the baby in the family had been usurped by Hap. Unsure of where I now fit in and missing Frances desperately, I began an endless search.

In my quest for a love to replace Frances, I turned to my mother, who before Frances left, had been merely a benign presence, a sweet perfume that drifted down the hall, a click clack of high heels on our polished wood floors. Now crying, clinging to her side, I hung on to her for dear life. Her soft fingers brushed against my brow. "Hush," she whispered, "hush. Any more tears and you'll fill up all the teacups in China." As she sat next to me in the darkness of my room, I calmed down under her gentle love.

Then I heard Dad's footsteps and his voice calling out to her, with my mother responding, "Prentis, I'll be right there." Quietly, she slipped from my side, leaving only a faint indentation on my comforter and my heart aching. Terrified that she, too, like Frances, might disappear from my life, I tried my best to be a good girl. I hid my sadness, not wanting to cause her any distress.

Even so, I couldn't help myself from writing my mother notes, writing what I couldn't speak, telling her how much I loved her. I left them for her everywhere, on her pillow where she would find them when she came home late from a party, on her bathroom sink where they lay wrinkled and soggy, in her dressing room drawers, even in the tips of her black satin evening shoes.

I don't think Mother understood the depth of my despair; in my memory she responded in a kindly, bemused sort of way to my urgent communications. She was never impatient, but neither was she as demonstrative and loving as

I wanted her to be. But I settled for whatever attention she gave me, knowing she could handle only so much of my neediness. Throughout my life a longing to be close to my mother stalked me.

With my buffer, Frances, gone, I was now more aware of how my mother interacted with my father. If she disagreed with him, he got angry. Many times I watched her quiet her voice, giving in to pacify him rather than standing up for herself. Forgetting about that solid little girl of Frances' days, I followed her example. Intuiting the danger in my family of being vulnerable and outspoken and knowing that my mother didn't want anyone in the family to upset my father, I now kept my feelings and opinions to myself; I learned to hide and be quiet.

When she was busy at her desk, I'd sit behind the heavy curtains in her bedroom and listen to the scratch of her fountain pen or her happy voice talking to friends on the telephone. At night I would walk in my sleep, finding myself in my parents' bedroom, shocked awake by my father's angry voice demanding I return to my room. The following night I'd be at their door again, but this time I'd find it locked.

My sleepwalking became extreme and I ventured further away. I went outside and roamed up and down our block. Later all that I'd remember would be the cold on my bare feet and the click of the lock that unlocked our front door. When I walked in my sleep, it was as if I were two people: one who was aware of certain small details that seemed perfectly normal at the time and the other who was swept along by some mysterious, unconscious force that wiped all reason away.

One night as I was returning from one of my forays outside, I felt a heavy hand shake my shoulder and heard Miss Cooke's voice. "What are you doing, young lady?" Startled awake and totally disoriented, I had no conscious sense of why I was barefoot, standing in my white cotton nightgown, downstairs by our open front door, in the middle of the cold darkness of night.

As I grew older, these nocturnal wanderings ceased except for two occasions that stand out in my memory. I was ten and sharing a room with my sister at the lodge at Sugar Bowl. I went to sleep in the twin bed next to hers; she was out with friends. Suddenly, a man I had never seen before awakened me, asking me why I was in his room using the bed next to his. I had no idea. All I remembered was seeing a bed turned down and thinking it was mine.

When he asked me my room number, fortunately, I remembered and he directed me back. The next morning when I came down to breakfast and greeted my parents, a man I didn't recognize asked my father if I were his daughter. Then the story unfolded. And only then did I remember the icy cold crunching of the snow under my bare feet and realized I must have walked along the outside porch that ran past the lodge bedrooms. My father didn't know whether to be angry or to shrug the incident off; he chose to make some joke about my being a bit too young to be chasing men. I blushed.

The other time I remember sleep walking was when I was 13 and in my first year at a boarding school in Connecticut, 3,000 miles away from home. I was lonely and missing California. All the students lived in a rambling, four-story building, each floor and four-girl room a replica of the next. Even the beds were in identical places to the ones on the floors above and below. One night I was awakened by a girl pushing me away from her, asking me why I was in bed with her. Momentarily confused, I then realized I had been sleepwalking and gotten the floors mixed up. I remember thinking, "Oh, someone is in my bed; no problem, there's room for two of us." With this incident, I needed to do a lot of explaining.

Much later I would understand that these night time excursions were my ongoing attempts to find Frances. But for the moment I only knew that I missed her deeply. I also knew that if I mentioned her name, my mother would be upset and my father would be angry. So I was silent.

But I never forgot Frances, carefully wrapping up the memories of my six years with her and storing them away in my heart. Once when I was about twelve, I nonchalantly asked my father if he knew where Frances was. "Frances?" he said. "Frances, oh, she's dead." He turned back to the newspaper he was reading and I didn't say another word, but somehow I didn't believe him.

Thirteen years later when I became a mother to my first son, Christian, my yearning to find Frances intensified and I began my search. On a certain level I was scared because I could not get rid of the feeling that Frances had left me so many years ago because of something I did wrong, because I was no longer deserving of her love. But my desire to see her again overwhelmed these doubts. I tracked down other families she had worked for after she left my parents' employ. My search led me to a trailer park in Sacramento, California, to 2211 Vagabond Way.

I called asking if I could come for a short visit. She sounded happy to hear from me. When I pulled up in front of her tiny trailer, with my son Christian, age six, by my side, I was trembling, so afraid that I was not worthy of her love. Perhaps, I thought, she wouldn't want to see me after all. I squeezed Christian's hand and slowly walked up the three stairs.

Before I could knock, Frances opened the door. Without a word, she reached out her arms and hugged me for the longest time. I just stood there, tears rolling down my cheeks. Hugging her back, I was gripped by a pain so strong that I felt as if I were suffocating; my throat ached and I could not speak. Again I was four and could feel Frances' strong fingers as she braided my hair, carefully tying a red ribbon with my name on it as a finishing touch. When I came up for air, I turned to Christian and introduced them. I realized he was the same age I was when Frances left.

Of course she was smaller than I had remembered, but when she smiled, her blue eyes alight behind her simple wire-rimmed glasses, her short red hair now streaked with grey, neatly curled, she still matched the picture I had etched in my heart. As Christian ran around, thrilled to be in this miniature house, Frances and I laughed and talked. "Do you have any pets?" she asked. "Oh, Linda, I remember when you were four, at school you were asked what you wanted to be and you said 'a mother cat with kittens'." Without a pause, she added, "Do you remember how you practically never cried? If you fell, before you hit the ground, you would say, 'It didn't hurt. It didn't hurt.'"

"And books, oh how you loved books. When you were two and three, you didn't take a toy or a blanket to bed, but always a couple of "Little Golden Books" and a few pencils. They were your security blanket. No, you didn't write in or mark up your books. Just pencils and books went together for you. As you fell asleep, one by one the pencils would drop onto the floor."

As I listened to her words, later writing them down to remember always, I suddenly understood that she had never stopped loving me. When I left that afternoon, I really did feel as if I were standing taller and walking with a lighter step. I even did a little dance as I unlocked the car. A few weeks later, she wrote me a letter and enclosed a picture of herself. "Tell Christian that I found his good-bye note in the little box outside my door. I can't part with it." She continued, "Linda, my fondest wish now would be for you to have a little girl just like you. You were so loving and intelligent; remember you are so very loved. Yes! I have always loved you so very much."

We never saw each other again. A few months later her sister called to tell me that she had died unexpectedly from complications with pneumonia. She added that Frances would have been 75 that August 12. That single letter and the snapshot are the only tangible evidence I have of Frances, but she gave me two irreplaceable gifts: tools to become the mother I needed to become and her love, which sustained me and kept me afloat through some stormy seas. As a mother to three sons, I have tried to love them in the many ways that Frances and my mother loved me.

When my son John was two, he had nightmares that sent him running down the hall to our bedroom. Jumping in between us, he would fall asleep. Remembering those times when I had slept next to Frances, I would reach over and smooth his soft, dark hair. One summer night, sitting by an open window with him in my lap, I sensed two pair of arms around me; not daring to move, I stayed there, John asleep against my breast, until the moon was high up in the sky.

Frances' loving presence in my life, however short, was both an anchor that grounded me and a compass that has directed me through this life, and I am convinced that our reunion gave me the strength I would need to eventually stand up to my father.

2

2920 Broadway

Without Frances, I felt my father everywhere. I remember his incessant lectures about the importance of family. He would press his thin lips together, narrow his eyes and say, "The only people you can trust are your family. Family comes first above all else. Remember, Linda, your actions, both negative and positive, reflect back on all of us. But no matter what, we will always love and support you."

His words took hold of my heart and I felt lucky and secure to be part of such a wonderful family, one I could turn to whenever the need arose. But without Frances, even at the age of seven, I began to worry about things I had never thought about before. How would I be able to live up to Dad's expectations? What if I failed or did something wrong? Would Dad stop loving me?

Sunday evenings, the cook's night out, we'd go to Maye's Oyster House, a dark, ornate restaurant with red leather booths. My sister and I wore matching dresses and black patent leather shoes. Once Dad asked me what I wanted for dessert. I couldn't decide, so I chose both the chocolate sundae and the crème caramel. He was furious and made a big scene, yelling at me and telling my mother that I was extremely spoiled. A feeling I had never felt before swept over me; I buried my head in my hands, trying to make this bad little girl disappear. Mom's words "Prentis, she's only seven!" floated over me, unable to reach me. It was Dad's voice that always rang the loudest.

Throughout our childhood, we were all afraid of him, a feeling that stayed with us until he died. Rather than bear the brunt of his unpredictable anger, we tried hard instead to win his approval, capitulating to his will to avoid reprisals. Scared to show any initiative contrary to his, we never dared to follow any dreams we might have.

Hilary, the oldest, always obeyed Dad's dictates, never standing up for herself or anyone else in the family. Rusty, the firstborn son, inheriting my mother's red hair and sensitive, creative nature, was more truculent. Yet he ultimately gave in to the pressure to follow in his father's footsteps, becoming a businessman rather than choosing a profession better suited to his creative talents. Until I was middle-aged, I, too, never dared cross my father. Well aware of his high expectations, I toed the line. I worked hard in school and in the outdoors, I competed furiously with my brothers, holding my own, riding, hunting and skiing with them.

Because my younger brother was raised by Miss Cooke, a somber, humorless English governess, he was somewhat shielded from my father. But she spoiled him. He quickly lost initiative to fend for himself, preferring instead that she do everything for him. Many breakfasts when the rest of us were having cereal and canned juice, Miss Cooke served Hap filet mignon and freshly squeezed orange juice. "He needs his vitamins," she explained crisply. She even peeled his grapes for him. Pretty much avoiding any direct confrontations with Dad, Hap instead played mah-jong with my mother and had his dinner brought to him on a tray in the T.V. room when his favorite show was on. Hap, the boy-king, the indulged youngest child, made us laugh, finding his place in our family as the court jester.

Over the years, Mom would sometimes try to intervene on our behalf, but ultimately she, too, caved in to my father, setting an example we all followed. If any one of us dared to express a view or desire contrary to his, he was furious and responded in kind; his will would be done. Once when Dad decided to go to the ranch for the weekend, I asked if I could stay in San Francisco for my best friend's birthday party. "Linda," he said, "how dare you spoil the family's plans? You are a very selfish young lady."

It was he who controlled all parts of our lives, down to the smallest details. He decided what schools we went to, what friends we should (or shouldn't) have, what skin products (Erno Laszlo) I must use as a teenager, what our extra curricular activities would be and what we should do on vacations. He sent my sister and older brother to summer camps he deemed the most prestigious. When my turn came, I asked if I, too, could go to camp. (I was interested in tennis and fervently hoped that I could go to a tennis camp of any kind and find some friends to play with.) "No," he said, "I want you near me. You'll be at the ranch. And I don't want to hear anything more – ever – on this subject."

True to form for a bully, he feared anyone who was strong and might be able to stand up to him. One tactic he used to fuel our insecurities was to set unreasonably high standards, knowing that often we would fail. "Live up to your potential," he would say. He was not satisfied if we did the best we could; to earn his "love," we had to be the best. When I brought home my report card with all A's and one B, he frowned and told me that Miss Cooke would sign it, not he. When I was elected vice-president of our eighth grade class, he wanted to know why I wasn't president.

A power broker and master manipulator, Dad admired Machiavelli, often quoting him: "The end justifies the means. Divide and conquer." With his intimidating manner he kept us under his thumb; fearful of being his next target we were always off balance. At times Rusty and I and later Hap, forged secret alliances, but they were made of paper, collapsing easily under his pressure. When he was being particularly unfair with one of us, we never collectively confronted him.

Knowing well that there was strength in numbers, Dad played us against each other. Usually he claimed me for his favorite, loudly singing my praises at the family dinner table, making me want to run upstairs and hide in my bedroom. Rusty, in particular, never forgave me for Dad choosing me.

However much my father said he loved me, I saw how mercurial he was, how little it took – one opinion, one observation contrary to his – to get on his bad side. One minute he was charming and expansive, the next mean and sarcastic. If anyone displeased him, he became cruel verbally, his cutting remarks humiliating us and reducing my mother and me to tears.

A capable cultural leader in San Francisco, my mother

put her role as a devoted wife and mother above all else. She believed, with all her being, in my father and in our family. She felt her marriage was her destiny. "It's in the stars; your father and I are meant to be." She added, "Each one of us has only one soul mate and I am so lucky to have found your father."

It was obvious to her children and friends that my mother loved Dad with all her heart; she called their marriage "a match made in heaven," often referring to him as Mr. Wonderful or Sahib. She was the heart and soul of our family, the spiritual arbiter. Although I always yearned for just a little bit more from her, she was clearly the one I loved best; I listened most closely to her. Touching us all with her softness, she never raised her voice or got angry with me.

Mom carried out my father's orders, organizing her children's many appointments, lessons and social activities while efficiently running three houses – 2920 Broadway St., our house in San Francisco, the HE ranch, our Sonoma retreat, and Sugar Bowl, our ski house in the Sierra Nevadas.

Every Monday morning my mother would meet with Gio, our talented (but temperamental) Chinese cook, to discuss the week's menu. Adrian, our gay French butler, hovered in the background, slamming cabinet doors, running water loudly in the pantry sink. He and Gio clashed over everything – who could read the paper first, who sat where around the kitchen table, or who washed what dish. They had clearly had yet another fight; storm clouds crowded the kitchen and my mother, once again, brokered the peace between them. Sending Adrian off to buy fresh flowers, an errand he loved, she diffused Gio's loud complaints with questions about what to serve for dinner.

She juggled many balls very well, managing also to be available for my father and supportive of whatever project or idea he had in mind. Like his mother, he loved to entertain and my mother organized dinners before the opera, ballet, or symphony, house parties at the ranch and cocktail parties honoring their many friends and their children. Studying the Great Books, my parents dined by candlelight with scholar Mortimer Adler where they argued endlessly about the ideas of Aristotle, Socrates and Plato, as Gee, Dad's houseboy and Adrian silently passed Gio's hallmark soufflés.

Forever on the move, always engaged in his business deals, his many boards, his architectural projects and our family, Dad was hard-pressed never to waste any time. "Grass never grows on a busy street," he joked, in reference to his baldness. He insisted that Mom be his constant companion and she was happy to oblige, putting his desires and needs before those of herself and her children. Already an excellent rider, she learned to hunt, fish and ski. Like his parents, they both loved to travel. Their many trips included going to the Fiji Islands to scuba dive, New York for the latest Broadway play, Kentucky for the Derby and France to buy Impressionist paintings.

Their travels weren't always easy for me, especially when I was younger. Once when I was about ten and they were about to leave on one of their frequent trips, I could hardly control the big, black shadow of sadness that roamed around inside me at the thought of my mother leaving again. When I saw Gee bring down their suitcases and put them by the front door, I walked away towards the large picture window that framed the Golden Gate Bridge because I didn't want my mother to see that I was upset.

Dad called out. "Linda, come say good-bye to your mother." I couldn't move; tears slipped silently down my cheeks. Hearing his heavy footsteps, I squeezed my eyes shut, hoping my tears would somehow disappear. When he saw my face, he became cross. "You should be happy for us; don't spoil our trip even before we've left," he said. Mom leaned down and hugged me and I buried my head in her soft jacket, hiding once again from that selfish little girl who couldn't decide on one dessert.

When my parents weren't traveling, they were always busy in San Francisco, where Dad had built up his image as a civic-minded business leader and family man. His energy was irrepressible. Not only did he serve as Chairman of Broadway Hale stores, over the years he was also a director of nine major corporations, including Union Oil, Santa Fe Industries, Syntex Corp. and Bank of America. He was president of the San Francisco Opera and member of the San Francisco Symphony and War Memorial boards. My mother was active in the community as well, serving on the ballet, opera and museum boards and also was appointed by Governor Pat Brown to the California Arts Commission. During this time they donated a beautiful Renoir portrait, *L'Algérienne,* and a Monet seascape to the Legion of Honor museum where my mother served as a trustee.

The job that actually brought my father the most status was a volunteer position as head of the organizing committee for the 1960 Winter Olympics at Squaw Valley. With obvious pride in her husband's accomplishment, my mother told this story. A week before the Squaw Valley Olympics were to open, it started to rain in the Sierras, ruining the snow, which, as it melted, flooded the parking lots. My father was in a panic. Finally, the temperature lowered and it started to snow – and snow – and snow.

On the day of the opening ceremonies, my father, over-weight at the time, was walking with Vice-President Nixon to the stage. Nixon dropped his fountain pen. Leaning over to pick it up, my father heard a huge ripping sound and realized his pants were now wide open to the wind. Nixon offered him his overcoat, which Dad gratefully accepted. As my father, with the borrowed overcoat slung across his shoulders, stepped up to the podium, the snow stopped, the sun came out and everyone cheered. "It was unbelievable," my mother said. "The angels were watching. Your father was magnificent."

I was 15 and 3,000 miles away at boarding school when a friend called to tell me that Miss Cooke, still my younger brother's governess, had shot herself. Even though I had never warmed up to her, I was shaken by the news. In tears I called Mom to ask what had happened and she brushed over this suicide, saying it was something we didn't need to discuss again. I felt both relieved and anxious.

The following summer when my parents were away on a trip, Adrian, our French butler, went into my father's study, opened the top dresser drawer and took out his pistol. Holding it to his right temple, he shot himself, splattering blood over the doors of my father's closet. Later Mom down-played his death also, explaining that he was not only temperamental but also troubled. But this second suicide in our household, coming so soon after Miss Cooke's, felt darkly familiar.

As if that weren't more than enough for one year, when my best friend from high school arrived for a visit that same summer, she immediately received a phone call from her father saying that her mother had just committed suicide. My mother simply took charge as she always did when helping others, comforting my friend in those first devastating moments, helping her absorb the pain such a death creates, comforting her with her strong arms and words.

Later my mother and I finally talked about Adrian and my friend's mother. I'll never forget her words: "Linda, suicide is not a solution to one's problems. Don't ever consider it." When my mother took her own life just six years later, I wondered how she could have forgotten her emphatic words so soon. Before her death, I believed all she had said to me, but afterwards the idea of suicide would seep into my psyche, filling me with its possibilities.

Despite all the traumatic events preceding my mother's death, throughout my teenage years we managed to keep up the appearance of the model family: two parents who were devoted to each other and four children who were extremely close. Dad still totally controlled us. Monetarily, he kept us all, including my mother, on a very tight leash. I had barely enough to cover my needs, but never anything extra for luxuries and every penny of my allowance had to be accounted for in my ledger book. If I bought a 35 cent coke at the Burlingame Country Club, my father's secretary would send me the bill. (Dad, notorious for checking every item on a restaurant tab, was a cheap tipper. After he left our neighborhood restaurant, sometimes my younger brother and I would sneak back and leave an extra dollar for the waiter.) I wore my sister's hand-me-downs and was eager to get a job in college to pay for extra expenses.

Dad was penurious with my mother as well. Even though

I grew up in a grand house staffed with many servants, I didn't understand that we had a lot of money because it seemed that my mother was uneasy about how we would manage. She would often sit at her desk trying to pay all the bills. Frustrated, she would sigh when she realized she didn't have enough money to pay the gardener. When my mother's Aunt Tanta died, leaving her small estate to my mother, Dad took control of those assets as well.

He used money to keep us in line in other ways too, gifting us with a small amount at Christmas if we were in his favor and withholding it if we weren't. Money was very important to him but not to my mother. Even though I received such mixed messages from my parents, I was used to budgeting and not being treated in a generous way. Like my mother, I never placed the importance on money that my father did. Later when I was married and sued my father to gain control of my trust, I asked not for any money but for independence and fair treatment. Instead he thought I was greedy and acquisitive.

When we grew older, Dad began to include us in many of his magical trips. We attended the opening of *The Pajama Game* in New York. We traveled to Paris, London and Rome. We fished for marlin in Baja, skied two spring vacations in Arosa, Switzerland, and spent a month in the bush of Mozambique hunting and camping, returning to Kenya two years later to shoot elephant.

On one New York venture when I was 17, Dad took me to the Wildenstein Gallery where he had three beautiful paintings by Bonnard on hold. Telling me to choose one, he went off to his meeting with the owner. Agonized, I was sure I would pick the wrong one, but he was pleased with my choice, hanging it over the fireplace in his study. "One day, Linda, this painting will be yours," he said later, draping his arm over my shoulders. I felt a wave a relief that I'd made the choice that pleased him.

Dad was an incessant planner. After finishing their dream house at the ranch, he turned his attention to the Sierras, where he and Mom built a lovely ski house at Sugar Bowl, an elite retreat three hours east of San Francisco. I particularly remember the spectacle we made. Arriving via gondola at the resort lodge, Dad would immediately start barking orders: "Linda, you and Hil go on over to the house with your mother on the Caterpillar; the boys and I will walk."

My sister and I, along with Mom, dressed in her leopard skin coat, Adrian in his gray butler's jacket, Gee in a high white collared coolie coat, Cocie, our Burmese cat, who was howling inside his wicker cage and Pepe, the white standard poodle (newly clipped), would all climb onto the open vehicle. Aside from the mountain of luggage and boxes of groceries, there would be the odd orchid or a paisley parasol poking out. Embarrassed that I might see someone I knew, I would crouch down behind Pepe and pull the collar of my parka high around my face.

Dad also remodeled an old brown-shingled boathouse at Lake Tahoe and started construction on a houseboat in Sausalito, another fancy place where he could entertain. (That one was never finished because of Mom's death.) In the fall during duck season, we traveled up to the duck clubs, one east and one west of the Marysville Buttes, the smallest mountain range in North America, where there was some of the best duck hunting in northern California.

In order to pass these holdings on to their children and

avoid estate tax problems, my parents placed these assets, including a lovely Berthe Morisot Impressionist painting, into a family corporation, Hilary Farms, which they set up to benefit us after their deaths. We, the four children, were the only shareholders. "This painting belongs to you kids," Dad said on more than one occasion. Rusty and I would often joke, wondering which quarter of the canvas we owned. At this time in his life, Dad was still a family man, determined to preserve and build up these assets for us, fully intending for us to enjoy them as he and my mother were.

He exposed us to so many wonderful experiences and provided us with myriad opportunities to see the world in great style, for which I am grateful. But everything was always on his terms, always under his complete control. We learned to follow his compass, not our own inner ones.

3

Behind the Façade

My father's need to insert himself in all aspects of our lives, including our emotional ones, was relentless. When my sister was 22, she had a very nice beau whom she loved but whom my father disliked. "He won't get anywhere in business," my father concluded and forbade the marriage. Instead he chose a Stanford Business School graduate for her, "someone with potential." When Rusty was 24, our father orchestrated yet another match, pushing my brother into a marriage well before he was emotionally ready to settle down.

When I graduated from Vassar College, without my father's knowledge I got an entry level job at McGraw-Hill. The salary was not enough to cover living expenses in New York. Excited about the prospect of living on my own, I approached Dad with the idea. Angry at the very idea that I might become independent, he insisted I return home to San Francisco. When I protested, he said, "Young lady, just how do you think you will be able to support yourself on that salary?" Then he threw in his zinger. "If you decide to stay in New York, you will not be a welcome member of this family."

I capitulated, returning home to 2920 Broadway. "I know what's best for you," he said. But really it was what HE wanted—for me to be the dutiful daughter, keeping my mother company when he left on his increasingly frequent trips and entertaining him when he was at home.

During this time I worked in a public relations firm, taking time off to travel on exotic trips with my parents—shooting partridge in Spain and pheasant in Czechoslovakia. I went through the motions of living my daily life, but I lost interest in pushing myself creatively or intellectually. Even though I found it harder than ever to breathe, laugh, or act in any spontaneous way, I pretended I was fine.

When I was 22 and my father was already involved with Denise, I became engaged to a young man with whom I had fallen in love at first sight back when I was 16. A close friend of my older brother's, he had spent a lot of time with our family either in San Francisco, Sugar Bowl, or at the ranch.

Unknown to me and for reasons I only later understood, Dad enlisted Rusty's help and together, the two men whose opinions I most valued (other than my fiance's) initiated a campaign to sabotage this relationship. Looking back I should have been forewarned then about my brother's character, so willing was he to undermine both his good friend and his sister.

Suddenly, my father became very interested in religion, surprising me, because that had never seemed important in our family. We had always been lazy Episcopalians. Expressing strong concerns over my fiancé being Catholic, Dad asked me if I knew I would have to raise our children in that tradition. "You'll have more problems than you know," he warned, narrowing his dark eyes.

When he asked how my fiancé would support me since he was in graduate school, I didn't have an answer. In one of many interrogations he expressed outright his disapproval of the match. "Linda, you should give more thought to choosing someone who would better fit into our family." I was surprised he said this, as in the past everyone seemed to like my fiancé. He was smart, well-educated and his parents were great friends of my parents.

Then my brother began making fun of my fiancé, giving me the impression that he also disapproved of this match. Emotionally needy and confused, I relied on his support and approval; when he seemed to agree with my father's stance, I began doubting myself. My mother, overwhelmed with her own problems, gave me no advice and said nothing in my defense. Within my family I couldn't find any advocates. Too insecure to follow my heart, I broke off my engagement to the man I loved, following in my sister's and brother's footsteps.

Later – much later – I understood the reasons why my father opposed this marriage. I think he realized that the potential status this marriage would bring me, both socially and financially, might make me too powerful. His position as top dog would be threatened and he would have little control over me and my potential husband. (This he could not tolerate.) Unless he personally benefited and still kept control, he wanted his children's spouses (in a *Chronicle* article he is quoted as referring to them as "hired help") to be subservient and malleable.

Flushed with his success, Dad asked me to go skiing with him. We rode up on a chair lift at Sugar Bowl. This was the concrete moment when I learned about his relationship with Denise. Turning to me and putting his arm tightly across my shoulder, he said, "I was with Denise in Los Angeles last week. When I told her you had broken your engagement, we opened a bottle of champagne to celebrate. Linda, I'm proud of your strength."

I didn't trust myself to acknowledge his admission or to say anything in response because I would have cried. I knew and he knew, also, that I was weak, not strong; with my silence I acknowledged that he had gotten his way once again. He was the winner. Meanwhile, stripped of my power, I felt ashamed; I hated myself.

Dad had just begun his affair with Denise Minnelli, then wife of Liza's father, Vincente Minnelli, whom he had met at a dinner party in Hollywood. Emotionally, I was a wreck after breaking off my engagement and I distanced myself as much as I could from what was happening to my parents' marriage. My mother, too, stuck her head in the sand until Dad's indiscretion made it impossible for her not to know.

Denying the affair to my mother but making no effort to cover his tracks, he would stay away for days at a time. Los Angeles gossip columnists mentioned sightings of them and all San Francisco society was talking about the affair and the marriage that everyone had thought infallible. Finally, my mother admitted to a few close friends, never to me, that she knew what was going on.

With Mom preoccupied with her marital problems and Dad never home, the household took on a subterranean life.

One weekend when both my parents were away, I returned early from a weekend at Lake Tahoe. Walking down our long front hall, I heard music and laughter. In our dining room, I saw that our table was set with my mother's best china and silver, while in the kitchen, Gio was grumbling and sweating over a hot stove. Nat King Cole's music was drifting through the speakers.

Puzzled, I entered the living room to find only men, but all were dressed up in women's clothes. They were drinking champagne and admiring the Impressionist paintings, with Berthe Morisot center stage. James, Adrian's replacement, swished to my side in what I realized was my mother's best black-satin opera gown. Then it dawned on me that they were all wearing something from my mother's closet.

Weaving unsteadily in my mother's high heels, James was obviously drunk. "Miss Linda," he slurred, "Stay, meet all my friends." Appalled, I ran up to my room and locked the door. Several times he pounded, begging me to join the party, but I refused. Two days later when my mother returned, I told her this story, fully expecting that she would fire James on the spot. Instead, she shrugged. Given her usual meticulous standards for running the household, I was shocked at her indifference. Obviously, our family household was beginning to unravel. The phone rang, she answered it and we never again talked of what happened that night.

Later her best friend told me that what devastated my mother as much as the affair was the collapse of her belief in Dad's integrity. Throughout their 33 year marriage, he convinced her that he had never lied to her. "The one thing I always knew I could count on was Prentis being truthful to me," she had said to her friend. "Now I don't believe him anymore."

But she was not yet ready to give up and kept going through the motions to keep up appearances. I'll never forget the night she readied herself for an opera dinner my father planned at our house on Broadway Street. (Renée, Mom's French maid, had told me Denise would be one of the guests at the party.) That afternoon, I arrived home from work to see a florist delivering a bouquet of flowers that filled our entrance hall. Renée received them.

Suddenly, my mother appeared and reached for the card. Seeing they were from Denise, she paled and then quietly said, "Here, Renée, I imagine these would look lovely in your home. Please enjoy them." Without another word, she turned away, her back straight and walked upstairs to dress for dinner. Although my heart broke for her, I didn't know how to talk to my mother about something as painful as this. Maybe by saying nothing, we both hoped Denise would go away.

It was hard for me to imagine Mom's agony that night. How could she sit there with her head held high, observing my father and Denise in the full bloom of their affair? Did she still believe it was only a passing fancy? Always in the past, appearances were of utmost importance to my father and so this flagrancy most likely forewarned my mother that she had lost the battle to save her marriage.

Mom never let down her guard with me, however and secretly I was relieved. After breaking off my engagement, I was in too painful a place myself. In the eye of my own emotional storm, I could hardly cope with my heartbreak. Had my mother reached out to me and asked me for help, I doubt whether I would have been much comfort. Still living on

Broadway Street, I'd given up any semblance of independence and was worn down. Although I loved my mother, I could barely fight my own battle. I just wanted out of the house.

Soon I was engaged to another man whom Dad approved. My mother threw herself into the wedding plans, a momentary distraction and something she hoped might bring Dad back to her side. On the day of my marriage, Dad and I went together to the church. For some reason during the brief ride in the limo, he decided to tell me of all the times he had been unfaithful to Mom. Desperately not wanting to hear, but once again not being strong enough to tell him to stop, I sat quietly, listening to his confessions, my mind blank and wordless.

I knew he was rationalizing his current affair by telling me of his many indiscretions, but I didn't feel sympathetic; I just felt like a granite wall. As we pulled up to the curb in front of the church, his parting shot was "And I bet you won't last five years in your marriage before you have an affair." I pretended I didn't hear him. Walking down the aisle with my father at my side, I could barely put one foot in front of the other.

Returning from our honeymoon in Jamaica, I checked in at 2920 Broadway Street. When I arrived, Mom was in the living room with one of her friends. After we hugged, I sat down to chat. Asking us to wait a minute, Mom went upstairs. She returned with all the jewelry Dad had given her over the many years of their marriage. She spread it out on the couch, touching each piece, reminiscing about the occasion of each gift.

Uncomfortable with her uncharacteristic behavior but unwilling to question it, I left soon thereafter. Thinking back, however, I understand now that she was trying to convince herself – with her friend and daughter as witnesses – that Dad once loved and cherished her and still did.

I never saw her alive again. Two weeks later she was dead. One of her closest friends told me Mom had been sure, because of Dad's power and influence, that no lawyer in San Francisco would dare represent her in divorce proceedings; she also feared that Dad would rally all of us against her. There she would be, alone and powerless, abandoned by her family, the very people Dad had promised her throughout the years of their marriage would never leave her side.

The night my mother died, Alex Brogle, her beloved ski instructor, was up in the Sierras at Sugar Bowl. There was a full moon, he later told me. Something drew him to walk outside onto his porch and as he looked across the snowy expanse, he saw three coyotes sitting in the center of the meadow. They lifted their heads towards the moon and howled for a long time. Never before witnessing this kind of behavior in all the years he spent in this mountain resort, he went to bed uneasy, awakening the next morning to the news of my mother's death being broadcast over the radio.

I'll always remember moments like the one when I was eight, when my mother said, "Come with me." And I followed her, down our long hall, into the warmth of her bathroom and sat by her bathtub as she bathed. Afterwards, I hid behind the dress I knew she'd wear that evening, feeling its silky smoothness against my bare arms. I slipped my tiny feet into her new black satin heels and pretended I was my mother, preparing to go out to the opera. I felt important as I helped her fasten the ruby and diamond bracelet Dad had given her for her birthday. She kissed me good-bye and I stayed in her closet for a long time, surrounded by the fragrance of her perfume.

In life my mother was brilliant and talented – an accomplished pianist, a perceptive intellectual, a linguist, an expert horsewoman. Her graceful energy and loving heart attracted everyone. After her death I lost count of the times her many friends told me, "Oh, your mother, she was the most amazing woman, always thinking of others, always trying to help out in difficult times." But above all else, she defined herself first as my father's wife and then mother of their four children.

When she died suddenly without our having a chance to say good-bye, I mourned not only her death but also the incompleteness of our relationship. I felt guilty that I hadn't gone back after she'd shown me all her jewelry to ask her why she had done this. I often wondered if I could have said or done something that last day I saw her alive that would have lifted her despair and perhaps prevented her death. I blamed myself and blamed my mother. I was ashamed and angry. Unable to imagine her final seconds, I was also shattered that so gentle a woman could die violently, contrary to her nature and all she stood for.

Before she died, my father would often wax enthusiastic about their wonderful marriage, his words contributing to this careful image he cultivated. In my gullible youth, I bought everything he said and perceived him to be the consummate family man, devoted to his wife and only wanting the best for us. Only later did I see beyond to the willful, duplicitous man who broke all the rules at the same time he was projecting a perfect family image. Growing up, I wondered how I could recreate a marriage as happy as my parents' and worried incessantly that I would never find that one mate meant for me.

Why would Dad have had to make such a big deal about how happily married he was and how great my mother was in bed? Why was he telling us and others how much he loved her when behind her back he was womanizing like crazy? Did he put her on a pedestal and then rarely touch her in bed?

I am sure that in the early days, their marriage worked, with Mom's loving nature tempering Dad's more narcissistic one. Her gentling influence reminded my father of what was good and right. But as they grew older, Dad began mingling more with the jet set world, leaving his old friends behind. He forgot about Larry, his first duck hunting buddy and shot instead with royalty in Europe, inviting then Prince Juan Carlos of Spain to be his guest at the ranch.

Recently, an old friend of my parents told me, "I liked both your parents," he said. "You know your father was not the most charming guy in the world, but your mother was a class act. She smoothed his rough edges." He continued, "I always thought Prentis was very lucky to have such a loyal, loving wife. She gave her whole life to him; he could do no wrong. She was so dedicated to him."

The year before my mother died, my parents hosted a party honoring Hayley Mills, a young Hollywood actress. That night my father circled our living room, kissing powdered cheeks and saying the same thing to every woman he touched – "You look marvelous, darling" – as he glanced over her shoulder to the next person he hoped to impress. He started taking more "business" trips, often now leaving my mother behind. Seduced by that surface world of appearance, money and power, he was losing interest in my mother and her values of the heart, a change that would continue well after her death.

What drew my parents to each other? Why did my mother choose to love a man like my father? What did my father most love about my mother? Instead of bringing out the best in each other, why did these parents of mine end up self-destructing? Why did I know so little about my parents' childhoods and even less about their parents? I longed to understand more about them and my role in our family drama.

As a child I would pester my parents for information about their families. "Stop," my mother would say to me. "You ask far too many questions." Only after her death, for instance, did I learn from her best friend that she had a genius I.Q. and was part of a study by Dr. Lewis Madison Terman, a Stanford University professor interested in these prodigies, whom he called "termites," a play on his own name.

Both grandfathers died before I was born and I can count on my fingers the times I saw my grandmothers. I had a scrapbook my paternal grandmother filled with newspaper clippings of her life, a handful of letters my mother wrote to my father before they married and some photographs. Beyond that, I was left to make sense of their reluctance to speak of their family relationships. I add their silence to what facts I know, to paint my picture of our family.

Three years after my mother's death, I would become a mother myself and would desperately desire not to repeat my parents' behavior. I wanted to be as healthy a parent as I could. And so, I searched.

4

Looking Back

My mother was born into a family of musicians. Her grandfather, F. Loui King, founded the King's Conservatory of Music in San Jose, California, in 1850, making San Jose one of the most illustrious centers of the musical world. He attracted pupils, including many talented solo artists, from Oregon, Idaho, Colorado and other states west of the Mississippi. A great teacher and composer, F. Loui King envisioned building up "the greatest musical center in America, if not in the world ... a center like Bayreuth."

In looking at his portrait, I saw a strong jaw and stern, piercing eyes staring back. Once my mother told me how much she loved sitting on his lap and stroking his full red beard. Clearly she adored her bigger-than-life grandfather, who died when she was young, a strong but brief presence in her life and one that encouraged her love of music.

An only child, my mother, Marialice Patricia "Pat" King,

was born in San Jose to Dorothy "Dottie" and Frank Giorza King, son of F. Loui King. A music instructor, composer and pianist, Frank worked under the shadow of his exacting father, teaching at the King's Conservatory. I never ever heard my mother speak of him and all I found to convince me he existed was a piece of sheet music in the bottom of her piano bench, "Impromptu in F," that he wrote in 1935. When I asked a friend to play it, I was mesmerized by its complex emotional brilliance. From him my mother inherited her skills as a classical pianist.

I heard a rumor that Frank committed suicide and before my father and I stopped speaking to each other, I asked him how my maternal grandfather died. "How am I supposed to remember that?" he answered in a cranky voice. "Maybe he stepped off the curb in San Francisco and was hit by a car. I really have no idea."

I can only conclude that my grandfather had been far from a solid father figure for my mother, probably receding more into the background of my mother's life after he and my grandmother, Dottie, were divorced. I suspect my mother had a problematic relationship with her mother, Dottie, as well. She never spent a single holiday with us and I remember seeing her only two times. (My mother was much closer to her father's sister, Tanta, who had no children of her own and adored my mother.)

Once when I was four and dancing to "Peter and the Wolf" while my nurse Frances was clapping, a woman I didn't know walked in. I stopped. Frances said, "Come, give your grandmother a hug." I did, but then I refused to dance again in front of her, despite Frances' urgings. There was just one other time, a night when Frances was on her day-off. I was in the bath and my grandmother, Dottie, washed me. I remember the smooth, soapy touch of the washcloth sending shivers down my back.

When I was eight, in bed with a severe case of the mumps, Mom came into my room. She was wearing a new grey wool skirt with a matching cashmere sweater and a single strand of pearls around her neck. Holding her cat Sinka close to her chest, she seemed distraught. Her eyes were puffy and her red hair, normally set perfectly in place, was messy. "Dottie's just died," she told me. "Dottie's gone." After that day my mother never again mentioned her mother's name and I didn't either.

My father's story was emotionally complicated as well. He – Prentis C. Hale Jr. – was the only child of Prentis Cobb Hale. The senior Prentis Hale was a bachelor until 50, when he succumbed to the charms of my grandmother, Linda Hoag Bryan, a divorcée with three older children – ages 18, 16 and 14. A department store heir, whose grandfather, Marshall Hale, founded the dry goods firm of O.A. Hale & Co. in 1873 in San Jose, Prentis Sr. was President of what became Hale Bros. Department Stores, the family business that defined him. He also served as vice-president of Bank of America, was a strong supporter of the opera and a member of the Pacific Union Club and Bohemian Club. A prominent, respected San Francisco businessman, he died in 1936, at the bottom of the Depression, leaving the majority of his estate to my father, then 26 years old.

My paternal grandmother, Linda Hoag Bryan, was powerful in a different, more extroverted and social way. Before she met my grandfather, she had made a name for herself in San Francisco as a gracious hostess and a well-known society and community leader. During the Spanish American war, she helped soldiers, an interest that led her to head up the Red Cross Canteen at the Ferry Building in World War I.

In the 1906 earthquake she saw the devastating effects of the fire, quickly setting up a clothing and food station in the basement of her 2422 Buchanan Street home for the wives and children of the firemen. Later she was voted an honorary member of the San Francisco Fire Department and in appreciation for her kindness and generosity, they presented her with a lovely silver flower bowl and tray engraved with: "In appreciation of your kindness to our wives and children following the great disaster of April 18, 1906, and with our sincere wishes for your future happiness and prosperity. Members of the S.F. Fire Department. Burned district."

My grandmother kept a book of clippings of her life in San Francisco. In her pictures, she always looks strong and opinionated. Definitely not pretty, she was, however, attractive and stylish. When she became engaged to my grandfather in 1908, the headlines say: "Society matron of San Francisco, Mrs. Linda Bryan, will marry Prentis C. Hale, a wealthy scholar and philanthropist." After their wedding they traveled by car down to Los Angeles, where they both had many friends. Even though I read that my grandfather had spent much of his life in Europe, their future home was in San Francisco, where "Mr. Hale's business interests are very large and where the popularity of his bride has qualified her as a social leader."

At first glance, my grandparents might have seemed an odd match, but I imagine their marriage worked. My grandfather, older, conservative and introverted, liked the extroverted energy of his younger wife who entertained beautifully.

Proud of her many achievements, he probably didn't mind that newspapers on both coasts reported their many activities. They hosted luncheons and dinners at their Woodside estate or in San Francisco, gathering interesting people from all over the world.

At their Mt. Shasta retreat, a day's train ride from San Francisco, my grandparents would have week-long house parties throughout the summer. Guests would play charades, croquet, bridge or tennis. A cousin tells me her father once watched tennis great Helen Wills Moody playing an exhibition match there. Near the swimming pool was a large lawn where guests competed in fierce croquet matches or sunbathed, wearing one of the many old-fashioned bathing suits from my grandmother's large collection.

During World War I my paternal grandmother's two sons by her first marriage served in the U.S. Navy. Hamilton, her oldest, entered Annapolis in 1909, became a Lieutenant Commander and was awarded a silver lifesaving medal by Congress for saving a fellow officer from drowning in Charlestown Harbor. Carleton, a law student at Stanford, enlisted, rapidly becoming a Lieutenant. Linda, the dutiful daughter, stayed near my grandmother's side, following in her mother's social footsteps.

Meanwhile, my grandmother's efforts at the Red Cross Canteen earned her the honor of becoming the first San Franciscan to be elected to the national board of the Red Cross. After the war she was also nominated by San Francisco's own Battery B, 347th Field Artillery, for being the city's most valorous mother. In a newspaper clipping from the *San Francisco Examiner* that my grandmother pasted in a scrapbook, I read: "Thousands of soldiers who passed through San Francisco on their way to war and after demobilization remember the kind-faced lady who presided over the canteen."

Aside from their philanthropic interests, my paternal grandparents shared many other pursuits. Both loved to travel and in 1921, together with young Prentis, my father, they spent seven months touring Europe. They also frequented the opera, entertaining their many friends in Box V. Both in their homes and in their gardens, they expressed their love of beauty, surrounding themselves with treasures – impressive collections of copper, silver and Persian rugs. According to a newspaper clipping, 6,000 hyacinths were blooming at one time in their garden on Vallejo Street in San Francisco.

My grandmother, a strong and devoted mother, was a champion for her three Bryan children, whom my grandfather welcomed into his life. But I am sure that he was thrilled when he learned he would become a father. Included in my grandmother's scrapbook is a small article entitled "The Stork on the Hale Roof" which heralds the news of my grandmother's pregnancy. "A very interesting piece of news which has just found its way here from New York concerns Mr. and Mrs. Prentis Cobb Hale, who are at present sojourning in the metropolis and is to the effect that the long-legged and busy bird, the stork, has perched on the Hale roof-tree, to the great delight of both Mr. and Mrs. Hale." On July 30, 1910 when my grandmother was 40 and my grandfather 50, my father, the heir apparent, was born.

Much loved and pampered by both parents, my father was certainly the center of their attention. His half siblings almost a generation older, he was raised (like my mother) as an only child. I imagine that Grandfather Hale, an older parent and by nature reserved, was not very involved with the rearing of his son, Prentis Jr. and left most of the parenting up to my grandmother, who was well-meaning but overbearing. In a newspaper picture of my grandparents and my father, taken in New York on their return from their seven month tour of Europe in 1921, I noticed that Prentis Sr. stood off to the side, self-contained and watchful. My father, then eleven, leaned into his mother, who draped her arms possessively around him. Clearly they were deeply entwined.

My father was precocious. My grandmother's scrapbook contains a clipping whose headline reads "Seven Year Old Boy is Wonder at Telegraphy." Apparently, after six lessons, he knew the Morse code perfectly, never confusing a dash or a dot and writing down sentences as his instructor spelled them. He also sent messages. "I have been in the business 15 years," Instructor Veyl says in the clipping, "and I have never seen any adult pick up telegraphy like this boy."

Although Dad was a mama's boy, he lived a far-from-sheltered life. Because of my grandparents' wide range of interests, he was exposed not only to the social, moneyed world of San Francisco, New York and Europe, but also to the remote, rugged world of the wilderness. Most summers he spent at the family's Shasta Springs retreat, at the base of Mt. Shasta, fishing, hunting and riding. The summer he was 18, he even worked in one of my grandfather's silver mines in Mexico, where he remembered the armed guards who protected the mines. Once a week, they all rode into the nearest town, two hours away, pistols in their holsters, ready to raise Cain.

Dad's outdoor experiences served to balance his city upbringing. Larry, my father's best friend for many years, told me a story from their duck hunting days. It was the early morning of December 7, 1941. My mother and Larry's wife had just driven two hours to their club, a remote shack out on the Suisun marsh, to deliver the terrible news. They located Larry, who rowed out to my father's duck blind. "Prentis," he yelled, "the Japanese have just bombed Pearl Harbor."

"Larry," my father is said to have answered. "Shut up. You're flaring all the ducks."

Defying school authorities, he was known as "a handful." He once blew up a school toilet with some highly flammable powder he stole from the chemistry lab. He was suspended more than once in his academic career, causing problems on the home front. By the time my father entered Stanford, he and his mother were definitely at odds. When she tried to control him through withholding money (a practice he would use later with us as well), he resorted to playing bridge and poker for high stakes, earning enough to get by. In college this future heir to the Hale Brothers department store fortune was a wild, rebellious maverick.

My mother presented a sharp contrast to my father. From what her Stanford friends told me, she was the campus star, smart and serious about learning as much as she could. She was also popular. I can picture her at her sorority, her high heels tapping with purpose down the hall, her lovely auburn hair curled in a long pageboy, perhaps a few books tucked under her arm. Her eyes were a lively brown and she smiled often. Her aura of warmth and capability were magnets that attracted my father, the rebellious loner.

I remember my father telling the story of their first date. Both were in the same English seminar and Dad, no dummy himself, had heard how smart my mother was. He had a long paper due in a few days. But he hadn't even started, so he invited her canoeing, and casually suggested she bring along her paper. When they were in the middle of the lake, Dad asked to see it. Standing up to hand it to my overeager father, she tipped the canoe and they fell, pages and all, into the lake. I never learned what grade he–or my mother–got on the paper.

The drenching, however, did not dampen their interest in each other and they continued to date. Linda, my grandmother, hoped for a much more socially prominent match for her precious son and was distressed at the inordinate amount of time the couple spent together. Hinting at disinheritance should they marry, she tried to undermine their romance any chance she could.

Her disapproval only made my father more determined to pursue my mother. They spent many weekends with my mother's beloved Aunt Tanta, a bustling, energetic, warmhearted woman, who was the only relative of my mother's who spent any holidays with us. Childless, she adored my mother and learned to like my father despite his contrary manner and lack of social graces. They also frequented the Hale family estate in Woodside, riding and picnicking under the august redwood trees that shaded this wild land.

After graduating, my father attended Stanford Law School. When my mother, still incurably in love, graduated a year later, she went to Europe for two months. (Undoubtedly, my grandmother hoped this trip would end their romance.) In letters that would later be given to me, my mother wrote to my father of her travels and of her love for him. A mixture of travelogue and yearning, they spoke of the depth and intensity I saw throughout my childhood of my mother's love for my father, which never faltered until the end of her life.

"Oh sweet," she wrote in one letter, "the thrill of seeing the Irish coast! We have been sailing through the Irish Sea today and I prayed that you were watching the same moon I was tonight. I was watching it make a path from Queenstown to me, while it was still two o'clock (P.M.) San Francisco time. The moon is almost full now and Wales looks beautiful from the boat. I keep thinking of Gladstone and then of 'Home Rule,' and I can just see that syllabus which we studied together entitled 'The Irish Problem' – and then I get homesick."

In another, she continued, "Oh please don't think I am a dreadful softy – but sometimes I don't think you know all you've given me. If you only knew the memories I have of you and Woodside – every time I look at the moon, I think of that last full moon I spent with you. You see, I remember everything and I know if I come back and find you completely changed, I still have something which you can't offer to anyone else. I can just see the way Woodside would look on a night like this. If I never go back there, no one can accuse me of not appreciating it while I had it, because I loved every minute of it and thought I was the luckiest girl alive. So you see I have something with you that some people live their whole lives for and still don't find."

When my mother returned from Europe, Dad was waiting for her at the dock. His father had just died, leaving his only child his entire estate, though his mother threatened to sue to get control of some of it. Although they settled this matter after a few months, this financial feud further separated them. Now that he was independently wealthy, he was no longer under my grandmother's power and free to do as he pleased.

Within a year, on September 17, 1936, my parents were married in a small ceremony hosted by Tanta at her home in San Jose. Dad's mother, furious that her son was once again disobeying her, was not in attendance. In a photograph taken on their wedding day, my parents both looked somberly at the camera. My mother wore a simple, white organza dress with puffy sleeves and a bow at her neck and was holding a bouquet of white hydrangeas. Behind her serious expression, her eyes danced with love. My father stood slightly behind her, standing straight in a blue suit with a gardenia in his lapel, his piercing dark eyes framed by heavy dark eyebrows. He looked like a shy professor.

After five years of marriage, Hilary, my older sister arrived, and then a year later Rusty was born. But my father kept his mother away from her grandchildren. Not until I was born three years later in 1945 did the ice begin to thaw. Two months premature, weighing four pounds, one ounce, I lay in an incubator unnamed for three weeks while my parents argued.

Mom wanted to call me Devon simply because she liked the name. Dad, strangely enough, held out for Linda, in honor of his mother, the very person with whom he had such a conflicted relationship. Of course he won. One of my mother's friends told me that when I was born, Dad showered Mom with presents – soft, silky negligées, imported Italian bed jackets – and filled her hospital room to overflowing with flowers.

Once I became my grandmother's namesake, we saw her

from time to time. She took my sister Hilary, my brother Rusty and me to dinners at the Women's Athletic Club, now the Metropolitan Club downtown on Sutter Street. And we visited her at her home, where Rusty and I raced to see who could be the first to climb up onto her four poster mahogany bed, the same bed that after her death, my parents put in their bedroom at the ranch. Plagued with a sweet tooth that I inherited, my grandmother had jars of candy that looked like collections of exotic, colorful marbles, perched on top of glistening antique tables. I would always leave with my pockets bulging with red and yellow sour balls.

Even though my grandmother lived just five minutes away from our home, I never saw her in our house and we never celebrated any holidays together. I never saw my father and grandmother together, nor did I ever hear him talking with her on the telephone or mentioning her name. Even after she died in 1952, leaving him the rest of the family estate, he never let down his guard to remember her in any way.

Used to a strong woman, my father looked for a wife who could protect him. Mother's many accomplishments and capable persona fooled him into thinking he'd found the woman he needed, but as the years went by, her gentle, loving nature in no way matched that of my intimidating grandmother's. Denise, on the other hand, turned out to be much more like his controlling, hard-nosed mother, someone who felt more familiar. (However, unlike my grandmother, who believed in preserving for the family the Hale fortune our mercantile forebears spent 120 years building up, Denise, to our detriment, did not.)

My mother, too, sought out a strong, protective spouse.

Fooled by my father's controlling and powerful persona, she thought she had found the solid father figure she needed, but in reality, she had married a weak, self-absorbed, emotionally absent man similar to her father. The only difference was that, unlike her own father, Prentis Jr. had money and social position to support him, which enabled him to keep up a powerful front to the end of his life.

Seeking qualities in each other that they had not claimed in themselves, my parents, without knowing it, brought to their own marriage patterns of relating they had learned from their parents. Wounded from what had happened in their own childhoods, they acted out their insecurities in different, harmful ways. My mother was not strong enough to believe in herself without my father by her side. Loving him dearly, she rarely stood up to him. He, in turn, bullied her, ultimately overpowering her.

Why did my father keep those early letters my mother wrote him from Europe so long ago? Was it possible that he forgot he even had them? Or did he tuck them away in some safe place, not too far out of sight, so he could look at them now and then? Did their presence reassure him that someone once saw and loved him just for his heart and soul?

5

Life at the Ranch

The place I felt safest in the world and where my family was at its best was at the ranch, a wild, beautiful, 10,000-acre piece of land two hours north of San Francisco that my parents bought in 1947. In my first vivid memory of our drive up there, we all piled into our red, wood-paneled Ford station wagon, my father driving, my mother across from him with her knitting and crossword puzzle. Hilary, Rusty and I, with Frances by my side, sat in the back. Soon lulled to sleep by the steady motion of the car, I didn't awaken until we were on the narrow county road that snaked its way along Sulphur Creek.

The sun was setting, casting dark shadows over the huge, glistening boulders that lay in the river, looming unexpectedly from the depths of the gorge. I was excited because I knew we would soon be there. Slowing down to cross the last cattle guard, my father counted the coyote skins the foreman had hung on either side. He was happy. "Bob's shot ten of them; that'll keep them out of the sheep for awhile," he said.

We swung left onto a dirt road that led to a modest ranch house. Though six years later we would move up to what seemed like the edge of the world into a wonderful, big-beamed, wooden-floored, adobe ranch house that looked out over 10,000 acres of wild land, for now my father was content to stay here where our life was simple.

A grape arbor shaded us from the unrelenting heat, and a vegetable garden, with plump, ripe tomatoes, summer squash, zucchini and rows of corn that the chickens ran through provided us with fresh vegetables. Old enough now to go alone to the coop to collect the eggs, I was scared of the Bantam hens' sharp claws and always asked Rusty to accompany me.

Wrapped around the back side of the house was a large, screened-in sleeping porch for us kids and our friends. I remember the first time I slept there, a trial night away from Frances' room. I stayed awake as long as I could, comforted by the rhythmic song of the crickets and the rustle of leaves in the live oak trees. I watched the full moon, huge and orange, rise over the far-off mountains, illuminating the shadowy landscape with a magical light and turning our Sulphur Creek into a silvery, shimmering thread.

In the barns down the hill from the house, we kept an odd collection of horses. My father's stallion, Diablo, a dark, fierce, muscled stud, stood guard over his domain. My mother's horse, Dune, was a gentle, white Arabian. Barney, an ancient, ugly gelding, belonged to Jim, our caretaker, a World War II vet who came with the ranch and whom I loved with all my heart. Flicka, the newest acquisition, was a beautiful, yearling thoroughbred, the light of my mother's eyes.

Every morning, carrot in hand, I would rush down to see Flicka. When she heard me coming, she would nicker and walk slowly out from her stall. Leaning over the fence, I'd open my hand flat, feeling her prickly whiskers on it as she nuzzled me to get the carrot. One day she took longer to come out; I saw she stumbled slightly, as she haltingly made her way towards me. Mom was suddenly by my side, anxiously looking into Flicka's eyes and rubbing her neck. Bob, the foreman, whom I knew my mother disliked, slouched nearby. She asked him what was wrong, but he shrugged, turning away.

Later that afternoon, I stood next to my mother, who was hanging up the last piece of freshly washed laundry to dry in the sun. Suddenly, Bob's mongrel dog ran through the shirts, jeans and sheets, dragging some with him and knocking the rest onto the dusty ground. She was upset, calling out sharply to Bob to control his dog. The next thing we heard was a single shot. Running around the corner, we saw Bob, pistol in hand with his dog, dead at his feet. "I hope you're satisfied." His voice was ragged and his gait unsteady.

Without another word, my mother took my hand and we walked away. That night at dinner I sat as still as possible, watching the shadows from the kerosene lamps flicker across my parents' faces as they argued about Bob. The next time I was at the ranch, Flicka was gone and so was Bob. I came upon my mother sitting under the grape arbor, crying quietly and I climbed onto her lap. She rocked me back and forth, but she didn't tell me why she was crying. Somehow I knew not to upset her further by asking any questions.

Years later, I found out from Rusty that when Bob was drunk, he used to go to the barn when we weren't there and hit Flicka as hard as he could over the head with a whiskey bottle, finally causing enough damage to blind her. She had to be put down.

Another scorching hot summer day when I was four, my brother and I walked across the county road. Our toes pressed into the softened asphalt of the deserted county road that wound along Sulphur Creek, its ultimate destination The Geysers, some thirty miles away to the east. We waited in the shade of a large bay tree for Frances to come with our picnic. Bored, I spied what I thought was a pile of rocks and I made my way towards it, intending to jump over it. Suddenly, my seven year old brother pulled me back, telling me "No, no, it's a rattlesnake." Luckily, I believed him.

We spent many hours by the river, surrounded by the pungent smell of skunk cabbage. When I waded into the warm water, searching for salamanders, I felt the softness of the yellow moss between my toes. Once when I was splashing around, I saw a rattlesnake swimming nearby, seeking the coolness of the bay trees that lined the far bank. Rusty skipped stones across the quiet surface, a red-tailed hawk cried its sharp, lonely cry and I lay back on the warm rocks, the happiest girl in the world.

Mornings before it got too hot, my parents would go for a ride, my father on Diablo, the horse's dark muscles rippling, sharp hooves digging into the dust and my mother on Dune, following, an old felt cowboy hat shading her sweet face. For the longest time I would watch them until I saw only two small dots in the distance, one dark and one light.

While they were gone, I would ride Barney around and

around in the ring with Jim watching me. One day upon their return, my father told me I was ready to ride from the river back to the house without a lead rope. I was both thrilled and terrified. Later I looked at a snapshot Frances took of me riding Barney beside my father. We were a ways off, following a path beside the river. I was sitting up very straight and though I could not see our faces, I was certain I was smiling.

It was a summer day in 1950. Heat surrounded us, sabotaging any outdoor activity. Keeping one ear alert for the sound of the jeep that would herald the return of the men from their deer hunt, I wandered into the kitchen, happy to be in the dark coolness of our house. My bare feet stuck to the linoleum floor. My mother was at the sink, her red checked apron tied neatly around her slim waist. Sitting down at our small, round dining room table, I watched as she sliced white peaches, the juice dripping off the end of her knife. I pushed our Lazy Susan, the salt, pepper, ketchup, mustard and a china bowl of sugar spinning around in front of me. "Be careful, sweetie," my mother called out. "Don't upset the kerosene lamps."

Suddenly, the sound of tires crunching on the gravel came through the window and I rushed outside to greet my father, brother, Mr. Metcalf, Lawton, my father's best friend and Jim, an expert deer tracker. They unloaded a dead buck from the back of the jeep and I touched his antlers. The sharpness of the tips surprised me. Hoisting the deer high up on the side of the fence near the barn, they stood back to look at their prize. Somehow Mr. Metcalf managed to hook his legs over the top rung of the fence and he hung, upside down next to the carcass. Everyone laughed. Handing me a rifle, Dad told me to stand next to them, so he could take a picture. To this day I keep this photograph in my small album. Squaring my shoulders, I stared into the camera, excited to be a part of it all.

Guns were always present in our life. Dad was an outdoors guy, a man who loved to hunt deer and shoot birds. At age 8, Rusty already had a rifle, a .30/30 of his own and I had my eye on Dad's .25/35, peep sight, lever action, a rifle I hoped I would be able to use when I turned ten. I spent hours practicing with a .22, shooting at cans my brother set up behind the fields of corn. One evening Dad piled us in the jeep, driving us to Cloverdale, then a sleepy town with one small movie theater. Careening onto Main Street, he shot his pistol in the air, making sure everyone knew we had arrived and reminding him, I was sure, of his silver mining days in Mexico.

We needed more water on the ranch and so Dad consulted Jim Moss, the caretaker. A man of few words, Jim was big and cumbersome but gentle like his name. Well known as a water-witcher, he was able to find water where no one else could. Holding the ends of a willow branch he'd carved in the shape of a V, he walked all over the ranch, stopping only when the branch quivered and bent in his hands towards the ground. "Here's where you should drill the well," he declared to my father.

Skeptical, my father grabbed the stick from Jim, but when he held it, it didn't move. "I betcha ten bucks there's no water here," my father said.

"Sure as that buzzard is circling overhead," Jim responded, "there's water." When the well was completed, clear spring water bubbled up; my father never doubted him again.

Since the house had no electricity, when night fell, my mother would go from room to room lighting the lamps. Scratch, the sound of a match striking, the smell of kerosene and magically the house was bathed in a warm glow that gathered us all together. Being the youngest, I went to bed first, inside with Frances, falling asleep to the sound of my brother and sister and their friends laughing and talking to each other out on the screened-in sleeping porch. My parents, Lawton and the Metcalfs sat outside under the grape arbor, drinking wine. The men talked of the day's hunt and where they might go tomorrow and the women whispered about their children, their laughter wafting through the hot night air. Their cigarettes pierced the darkness like fireflies.

Mixed with these magical memories of the ranch was one painful moment when I was six. I was feeling lonely, worrying about whether Frances, now absent, would ever return. Father took me on a hike, the very same hike that had been a favorite with Frances and me. Since our last time there, the foreman had grazed his cattle in those fields, so I had my first glimpse of cow pies, which immediately intrigued me. I found I could use them as stepping stones and I made up a game of jumping from one to the next without touching the dry grass beneath.

What I didn't know and my father did, was that they weren't all dried out. Some were a lot fresher than others. He later told me he was waiting for me to land on one that was soft. Eventually of course I did and I slipped and got cow manure all over me – on my jeans, my hands, even in my face and hair. I sat stunned for a minute and then burst into tears. My father laughed, saying, "How can anyone be so stupid?"

Suddenly I felt Frances nearby and even turned around to

see if she had by some miracle returned. No one by my side, but I remember clearly to this day the feeling I had of her presence. I turned to Dad and said in a loud voice, "How can you be so mean to such a beautiful little girl?" He didn't answer and we walked back to the house in silence. I later overheard him telling my mother how spoiled I had become because of Frances' influence and that it was a good thing he fired her. That was the definitive moment I knew for certain that Frances would never be taking care of me again.

A year later, leaving far behind the little house, with its grape arbor that looked out over a small corn field, its Bantam hens and kerosene lamps, we moved high up onto a bluff into the adobe house my parents had designed. It was the culmination of their dream to build an elegantly simple ranch house, reflective of the wild and beautiful land surrounding it. They told us that it was to become a family refuge, a legacy to us and to our children, to be passed on through the generations. The place where we gathered together family and close friends, it nourished our souls, connecting our hearts in more ways than anything else in our lives. It was also the expression of my parents' love for each other, their happiness spilling over into our lives to create wonderful memories for me.

My father masterminded the building and landscaping of the ranch house and grounds, while my mother decorated the interior, a loving collaboration that resulted in an unusual and beautiful home. In planning the entire garden, Dad insisted on color, masses of color. Possessing a keen sense of proportion and beauty, he transformed the bare grounds. In front, hollyhock, iris, stock and hydrangeas tucked beneath the oak trees greeted us when we arrived. Out back a spread of zinnias, fierce red, orange, lemon and pink heads bobbing in the breeze, complemented the more subdued roses that graced the rose garden he designed especially for my mother.

Everywhere Dad planted jasmine that climbed up the wooden beams and onto the sides of the house, outlining it in fragrance. And in the garden outside my parents' bedroom where the purple clematis had already taken hold, my father planned with the greatest of care. There he put my mother's beloved gardenias, so mornings when the sun would hit them and their sweet, heavy smell would drift through the window, my mother, lying in the very bed in which my father was born, would imagine she was in heaven.

He lined the length of the back porch with prickly green Meyer lemon bushes, so their spice-scented white blossoms could mingle with the sweetness of the gardenias and jasmine. Gee picked the ripe fruit, squeezed the juice and froze it in ice trays to use later for Dad's special lemonade. Around the pool house Dad planted grapevines whose tendrils clung to wires he'd strung to recreate the grape arbor he loved from the little house near Sulphur Creek. Wisps of entwined purple and white wisteria peeked through the arbor. In late summer when the grapes ripened, we made jelly that Dad spread over barbecued wild pigeons we had shot in the early morning.

Below the big house, steps made of railroad ties led down to the lawn that surrounded the pool. Beyond the pool, the land dropped off steeply into California wheat grass and purple thistle that sometimes edged their way into the civilized lushness of our garden. From every vantage point there was a view of wild mountain ranges, yellow grass and oak trees with Sulphur Creek a tiny sliver in the distance below and no sign of any other inhabitant as far as you could see in any direction.

In contrast to the bright, pungent complexity of the garden, the house, with its thick adobe walls, was simple, cool and above all welcoming. The living room, with its high-beamed ceiling and huge fireplace framed with rocks from the river, was the central gathering area. Even in the height of the summer heat, we always had a fire at night that added sparkle to the softly lit room.

Two large couches faced each other and there we assembled for cocktails. To the left was a gaming table for dominoes, cards or backgammon. And at the far end was a long wooden dining room table that seated my parents, us children and as many guests–theirs and ours–as were present. Lively conversation and wine-soaked laughter filled the air. After dinner we played charades, or Mom organized a bridge game and I watched for awhile, sitting quietly behind her. Most of the kids drifted out to the back porch. Some nights when the moon was full, we played croquet on the lawn near the pool and afterwards would go for a midnight swim.

To accommodate all our friends, there were two dorms, a boys' and a girls', located on opposite ends of the house. Each was a screened-in room with eight beds, reminiscent of the old sleeping porch of the little house we started in. Many nights I remember talking with friends until all hours, mostly about boys, not realizing that we had an audience until we heard scuffling and muffled laughter from outside. One afternoon, late, we came in from riding to discover that the boys had made a panty raid and all our underpants were hanging from the black oak tree next to our room. Before dinner when they were out target shooting, we snuck down and short-sheeted their beds.

Up at the ranch my father was a different person than when he was in San Francisco. He was kinder, more fun, less than vigilant. Other than my assigned chore and strict instructions about fire and gun safety, there were few restrictions. In contrast to the tight leash Dad kept me on in San Francisco, this physical independence was intoxicating and I took full advantage of my freedom, riding everywhere. My friend Lizzie and I would ride out early when it was still cool, heading over to the backside of the ranch. Once there we took off our shirts, leaned back on our horses and let the sun beat down on our bare chests. We rode that way for hours. Then we tied up our horses near the small spring above Fraser Creek and gathered watercress. As the sun began to descend behind the far mountains, we headed for home.

Always full of ideas, Dad would organize our annual hare and hound hunt, a game we played on horseback, deciding who would be on which side. The objective was simple: one team, the hares, given a half hour head start, tied ribbons on trees, bushes, fences, the most difficult places we could find, to leave a trail; the other team, the hounds, followed. The hounds then collected all the ribbons to find us.

I was always on Dad's team, the hares. Galloping off, we'd head over to the back of the ranch. To confuse our pursuers, Dad told Lizzie and me to ride off in another direction and make a false trail. We did and then tore back to catch up with the rest of the group. Dad led us, finally, to the shade of Fraser Creek, where we hid the horses behind a grove of bay trees and sat down to wait.

Drifting off under a thick blanket of heat, I was startled

awake by the sound of horses crashing through the manzanita above us. I saw Mom riding in front down the steep banks on Dune and I was happy we were found. Later after the heat subsided, my mother invited me to go for a walk with her. Thrilled that she chose me, I ran to her side. Picking her way gracefully downstream, she dodged boulders and ducks under sharp branches; I scrambled to keep up.

When we came to a place where the stream widened, my mother stopped. Turning towards me, she asked, "What color is the water here?"

"Blue," I answered, far too quickly.

One eyebrow was raised and she said, "Now, Linda, just look; really look." Ever since Frances left, I'd had doubts about myself. I was afraid that if I were to say "brown or red or yellow" which were the colors I really saw, that might be the wrong answer and I did not want to appear stupid.

I stared at the water for a long time. "Blue," I said, still deciding to stick with safest answer I knew.

She sighed. "Look closer, sweetheart, through the clear water. Don't you see the brown, yellow and red rocks below?"

I remember this incident so clearly because it was indicative of how insecure I felt. I wished I had been brave enough to answer with the more unconventional answer, with the colors I really saw. I knew I had disappointed her by my dull and ordinary observational skills, but I was too scared that she might leave me, just as Frances did, to risk any other response.

Many years later after my mother died, I had a dream. It was night and there was a full moon above us and we were together again at the side of a river I'd never seen before. She asked me what color the water was and this time I didn't even hesitate. "Silver," I said, "silver and gold." Smiling, she reached out and pulled me in close to her heart.

After that moment with my mother by the river, we headed back upstream at dusk to the others. My father called me over to sit next to him. Casting his line into a deep pool near where the horses were tied up, he said, "Here, Linda, hold my rod for a moment." As I did, I felt something tug. "Lift your rod, lift your rod." On the end I saw a small trout, fighting to get free, but I landed it. "Good girl," he said. "That's my fishing girl. I'm proud of you."

Thrilled to be my father's girl, I moved in closer to his side. As it grew dark, a full moon rose up over the Geysers. We saddled up for home, my horse Tickle, the fastest of them all, out in front next to my father. Galloping in and out of the shadows the moon cast through the live oak trees, from above we must have looked like a band of coyotes streaking through the night.

When I was eight or nine, my father gave me a hard-to-manage horse named Tickle, short for Tickled Pink. She was a high-strung thoroughbred, thoroughly spoiled by her former owner who lived in Southern California. Tickle had loved her mistress so much that she had followed her everywhere, even standing and at times sleeping under her window at night. Missing her terribly, Tickle now misbehaved, biting or kicking me any chance she got. Always in a bad mood, she was a handful, hard to catch, hard to saddle and bridle. Even though she had two foals after she came to our family, she never got used to her life on our wild, rugged ranch, so different from her sheltered past.

I dreaded every time I had to catch her. Our ritual rarely

changed. At the far end of the pasture, I saw her grazing. Holding a small bucket of oats, I slowly approached her, hoping that this time I could coax her gently over to my side. Sensing me, she lifted her head, flattened her ears, snorted and then immediately charged me at a full run. Indeed, she rushed past me, grazing my shoulder with hers. I held my ground and then followed her. Calling out her name, I rattled the oats in the bucket. At times this performance lasted as long as half an hour before I managed to slip a rope and then a bridle over her head. Momentarily tamed, she followed me up to the tack house where I saddled her. But as I tightened the cinch, I felt her sharp teeth bite into my shoulder. Until I was in the saddle, I was terrified. Once I was on her, though, she was on her best behavior, by far the fastest, smoothest, most beautiful horse on the ranch. With her first step, I forgot my fear and together, we flew like the wind.

I was told never to bring Hap into the pasture with me when I went to catch Tickle. One day, though, a blistering July day when Rusty and Hilary were away at camp, I, at twelve, was alone at the ranch with only Miss Cooke and Hap, age six. Dreading my upcoming ordeal with Tickle, I talked Hap into coming with me. In my best big sister voice, I told him to stay right by the fence. As usual, Tickle raced towards me and in my fear I forgot about my brother, who ran from the safety of the fence to my side. Lightening quick, Tickle struck Hap with her hoof, knocking him flat on the ground. I lifted up his torn shirt and saw a bloody slash down his entire back. Trembling, I took him back to the house and a very angry Miss Cooke. This was one of the few times I remember going against an adult's orders. Realizing

I had put my brother in a dangerous situation, I thanked the angels that I know were by our side.

My father's gift of Tickle was a double-edged sword. Secretly, I was pleased that he gave me this magnificent horse, but I was also distraught because she was so difficult to manage. There was no question that Tickle, in her new surroundings, was much too much horse for a girl of ten. But since Dad gave her to me and I was responsible for exercising her, I had no choice but to stand out there in the middle of the pasture, scared to death and hold my ground as she bore down on me. Perhaps, though, facing Tickle toughened me up, preparing me for the inevitable time when I finally found the courage to withstand the full force of my father's wrath.

After the incident with Hap and Tickle, my brother and sister came home from camp and my parents returned from a fishing trip in Montana. Our family was together again and I was happy to have company other than Hap and Miss Cooke. After breakfast and when I was finished sweeping the porches, I looked for my mother. Now that she was home again, I stayed as close to her as I could. I spied her off in her beloved rose garden. Her floppy straw hat shaded her porcelain skin and strands of curly auburn hair peeked out from under the wide brim. She moved deliberately through the colored tangle, clipping a rose here, another there, laying them carefully in the wicker basket that hung from her left arm.

"Can I help?" I asked.

"Here, sweetheart, I have another basket and some clippers just for you. I'll show you where to cut them so more roses will bloom." She guided my hand to the spot on the thorny stem of a fragrant pink rose. "Bewitched," she said.

"It's my favorite, the one I place on the table next to your father's side of our bed." I decided it was my favorite rose, as well. After a while I wandered off to cut more flowers elsewhere in the garden, gathering and arranging them in the back porch sink. Then I placed bouquets throughout the house that brought wild color and sweet fragrance into the cool, dim interior.

Before dinner we gathered together on the back porch. Dressed in a simple V-neck black jersey and silk pants, my mother, sipping her drink, told us what had happened to her cat Sinka that day. She had been in her rose garden when she heard what sounded like a sprinkler gone wild. The rat-tat-tat sound got louder and she was puzzled, for no sprinklers were supposed to be on at this time of day. Then she had spied Sinka crouched, ready to pounce on a rattlesnake he'd cornered that was rattling its tail as hard as it could. Before my mother could react, Gee, nearby, had chopped off its head with his hoe.

I sat near my mother, listening to her every word. My father laughed, my sister decided she must watch her step and both brothers nudged each other, secretly hoping to be the ones to find the next snake. Moments like this connected our family in simple and real ways. We were a team. My memories of the ranch were pivotal to the conviction I held of my family's potential, when I perceived my parents and the four of us kids as loving each other in the best possible of ways.

Life at the ranch gave us opportunities we'd never be able to experience elsewhere. It was August 1955. I was ten and deemed old enough to shoot my first buck. Although proud and excited about the prospect, I was also apprehensive because Dad insisted that we act courageous at all times. It was unacceptable to admit we were ever frightened.

Waiting by the jeep for my father and older brother, I clutched the Winchester .25/.35 that Dad had given me. All summer, anticipating this event, I had been practicing with Rusty's .22, knocking down beer cans. I had learned to bring the rifle up to my shoulder, tight against my cheek and squeeze, not jerk, the trigger.

What if I missed – or worse – only wounded my first buck? At ten I already understood my father's conditional love. Whether he loved me or not depended on how I performed. In preparing me for this act, he carefully explained that I must aim at the head, right below the antlers, in the neck, or in the shoulder so the bullet would pierce his heart. "Take no prisoners," he added. (Once I was grown, I'd realize that he had followed this philosophy in every area of his life.)

Late that afternoon as we were driving home in the jeep, we saw a buck on a far ridge. Sensing our presence, he started to run. I thought he was too far away for me to have a shot, but Dad said, "You're up, Linda." I realized I had no choice but to shoot. As I lifted my rifle, I forgot everything I had practiced; I didn't even remember putting it to my shoulder or sighting in on the buck. I just knew I fired and he fell. Later as we stood over him, my father was obviously proud of me and somewhat amazed. "Great shot! In the temple and he was running."

I felt it was sheer luck that I killed that deer; in a million years, I am sure I could not have duplicated that shot. But I was relieved because I was successful in Dad's eyes and with this achievement I had, for the moment, won his love. The thought of failing or not living up to Dad's standards terrified me; at that young age I was already hard on myself as well. When Dad congratulated me, I was happy. That evening at dinner, Dad retold the story of my shoot, praising me for making such an incredible shot. Glancing at Rusty, I tried to catch his eye. But he looked down at his plate and was silent. Uncomfortable, I wished Dad would praise my brother, too.

After dinner that night my parents and I took a walk down past the pasture where our horses grazed. The dark night sky was filled with stars. My father pointed out the Big Dipper, showing me how to follow the bottom two stars up to the North Star. "You'll never get lost if you know where north is," he said. A coyote howled off in the distance and I stepped closer to his side. Roughing my short, brown hair, he said, "You're not scared, are you, kiddo?"

Right then my mother laughed and he reached out and took her hand. "Oh, Prentis," I heard her say, "I am the luckiest woman in the whole world." I felt that way, too. Here, together at the ranch, we were momentarily safe, away from that society world of San Francisco my parents inhabited. The beauty of the wild land around us soothed my father's wanderlust and softened his sharp edges; here he was content simply to love his wife and four children in the best way that he could.

I always thought we'd stay intact, this family of mine. I used to picture us growing older together, sitting on the back porch at the ranch, holding each other's babies on our laps, laughing at each other's jokes, searching out the first star in the evening sky that spread across that beautiful land. Many times I think of my sweet mother and willful father and wish the outcome of their lives had been different.

These memories of the HE ranch that my parents bought in 1947 as a sacred retreat for our family and close friends have never faded. Wherever I have traveled, to the High Sierras, to the rivers in Montana, or the beaches of northern California, the ranch has always been there by my side. It has been my talisman, a lucky charm that has grounded me, reminding me of the times our family connected in real and loving ways.

Even though my father eventually left this beautiful family property to Denise, his second wife, who had already transformed it into a showcase, I would remain the guardian of my memories. I have often wondered what Denise thinks when she wanders through my mother's beloved rose gardens, or walks down the steps past the old boys' dorm to the pool. Does she ever feel the wind that rustles through the leaves of the black oak trees? Does she hear the quail calling? Does she see the evening star dot the twilight of the turquoise sky? All I know is that she couldn't have heard us yelling, when we arrived at the ranch and tumbled out of the old red station wagon onto the acorn-strewn porch, "Mom, Dad, we're here, we're finally here."

6

Rusty and Dad

Whenever my father called me, I ran to his side. Although at times he scared me, for the most part I enjoyed whatever we did together. When I was ten, he took me to my first opera, "The Flying Dutchman," we bet on horses at the Santa Anita racetrack and when a new Broadway Hale department store opened in Los Angeles, I stood between him and Ed Carter, his business partner, at the opening ceremony. At the ranch when we played croquet or dominoes, he always chose me to be on his team and whenever we rode, Tickle and I were near the front, right behind him. I was his outdoors girl, happy to be included in anything he planned.

In those years my father was very vocal about his feelings towards me, telling me often how great I was and how much he loved me. He – and my mother – told their friends I was his favorite child, the one most like him. While I was happy that he approved of me, I was ambivalent about his excessive attentions, worrying that I might not live up to his many words of praise. And I was always afraid he might find out that I was not the perfect daughter he believed me to be. His singling me out separated me from my siblings, causing my older brother, Rusty, in particular, to resent me. Still I tried to be the best daughter that I could and we had a smooth relationship until I was a teenager.

When I discovered boys, he was not happy. Charlie, my first boyfriend, gave me his I.D. bracelet, which I wore in secret until one morning Hap came into my bedroom where I was asleep, my bracelet on my wrist. He told my father, who ordered me to return it immediately. "You are not allowed to go steady with anyone, young lady," he said. Setting up strict rules for me socially, he lectured me on boys and sex ("Why buy the cow if you can get the milk for free?"). When my friends came over, boys or girls, his many questions and intimidating manner scared them.

Although Dad kept me on a short leash socially, at home he became more and more familiar with me. Our relationship changed; I went from being his buddy to a young woman who interested him in a physical way. At dinner he talked more often about sex, looking at me when he proclaimed Mom's prowess in the bedroom. "Oh, Prentis," she protested, "please don't say such things." Then he would turn to me, "Linda, sit up straight and push those bosoms out more. You're a sexpot." I was mortified. He insisted on teaching me how to dance. After dinner he would put on Frank Sinatra and take my hand in his, his right arm tightly encircling my waist. Pressing his check against mine, he would twirl me around the hall, often pushing his leg in between mine. It was totally embarrassing.

One summer at the ranch just before I left for college, I wandered out on the porch after dinner. There was a new moon, a silver sliver off to the west and the black night sky was ablaze with stars. I heard the screen door squeak and suddenly Dad was by my side. Grabbing my shoulders, he kissed me passionately. I pulled away just as Adrian arrived to place the coffee tray down on the wicker table. I was utterly shocked, but as usual I didn't say a word. We both pretended this never happened, but now I couldn't wait to leave for the East Coast. When I was 3,000 miles away from his relentless attention, I felt safer.

At college though I was physically removed from my father, I was still emotionally bound to him, reacting in unhealthy ways to my independence at Vassar. With the heavy weight of parental supervision lifted, I ran wild. I slept late, missed most of my classes, went from cum laude in high school to a C+ average and played bridge (when I was not sleeping or eating) instead of studying. I frequented the Vassar Pub, stuffing myself with hot fudge sundaes and vanilla malts. And I gained 15 pounds. As Christmas vacation neared, I panicked, wondering how I would lose enough weight to be presentable for Father.

Out of nowhere I came up with a way to control my weight. Every time I binged on sweets, I made myself throw up. With enough practice, it became easy; soon it was an almost daily – but secret – ritual, one I thought I had exclusive rights to. It never occurred to me that there was actually a name for what I did. When I arrived home in December, I was thin enough to pass muster.

By summer I had regained the weight and when I returned home in June, Dad pronounced "our" deal. If I got down to 135 pounds and kept my weight at that level for a year, he would pay me $500. (If, however, I couldn't do that, I would owe him $500, a sum which I didn't have.) Enlisting my brothers to be his watchdogs, he posted a list of foods forbidden to me. Should they catch me eating something fattening, he paid them a ten-dollar reward and I had the same amount deducted from my allowance. Sometimes I managed to "eat" that up before the month was over.

I became the family's cause célèbre. Dad sent me to Eileen Feather's Weight Salon, where daily I stood for an hour hooked up to a machine with a wide belt that encircled my hips, supposedly vibrating away the pounds. But as soon as my session was over, I rushed across the street to Eppler's to buy a bag of glazed donuts, eating them all at once. At home I became an expert at sneaking into the kitchen at odd times, usually late at night, to find the coffee tins Gio filled with his rolled lace cookies. In my desperation, I even ate whole cans of applesauce and long-forgotten jars of Hap's baby food (tapioca pudding was a favorite) that lined the back shelves of the storeroom.

Somehow over the summer, I managed to get down to 135 pounds and when this happened, Dad stopped weighing me every day on his scale. "I trust you to keep up your end of the bargain," he said. Slowly, however, I regained the weight; soon, I dreaded coming down to breakfast. Reading the paper and not bothering to look my way, Dad asked, "So, what do you weigh this morning?"

My answer was always the same. "135," I'd say casually.

One day, though, my mother looked up. "Prentis, there is no way Linda still weighs 135." By this time, my mother probably sensed she was losing her touch with my father; in retrospect, I suspect that by discrediting me, she subconsciously hoped to win him back. At that time, however, I couldn't believe I was hearing her treacherous words. Although I appeared calm on the outside, inside I panicked. My father turned to her. "Pat, I know Linda would never lie to me." To me he said, "Just to prove it, Linda, let's get you on my scale after breakfast."

"Sure thing," I said, wishing I were anywhere but at the breakfast table. For once I couldn't eat.

Following him up the stairs, I felt like yelling, telling him that I hated being humiliated by him. Instead I was silent. He weighed me in like a side of beef. "147 pounds," he declared, his eyes narrowing. "Linda, how could you be so devious? You know the one thing I ask of all you kids is total honesty – an omission is as bad as a commission – and here you've downright lied to me. You've let the entire family down with your behavior. Go to your room immediately."

Unable to defend myself, I walked past my brothers and sister, who stood silently in the hall listening to Dad's excoriation; they, too, didn't dare speak up on my behalf. Devastated by Dad's cruel words, I spent the rest of the day in my room crying nonstop. That evening Dad came in. I heard him saying, "I'll give you another chance, Linda." He walked towards me and I allowed his arms to encircle me in their steely grip. I was at once ashamed, repulsed and relieved.

The following summer I went with my parents and Hap to Africa. I was still struggling with weight issues. Hap and I shared a tent. Once we were settled, Dad barged in, handing Hap a huge tin of chocolate balls. "Linda's on a diet," he announced, "but you might enjoy these, Hap." As if as an afterthought he added, "By the way, Hap, you earn ten dollars every time you catch Linda eating one." Feigning indifference to hide my anger, I willed myself not to look up from the book I could hardly read. Already I could feel the round ball against my teeth and taste the rich chocolate on my tongue. All I wanted to do was eat myself away from my father.

In the heat of the day, Hap and I were resting before our afternoon hunt. Seeing he was asleep, I quietly reached over and opened the top of the tin, quickly shoving four chocolates into my mouth. Then I grabbed a piece of Kleenex and stuffed it under the remaining ones to keep the level stable. (Hap checked the candy religiously). Unable to satisfy my deep-seated hunger, I ate almost the entire can before Hap noticed. Later, when we were again back in the tent, Hap slowly picked out a chocolate. Feeling only Kleenex where candy should be, he suddenly understood. "You ate them all," he yelled.

"Yes," I said, "but you didn't catch me in the act. So you can't collect any money from Dad." Of course Hap reported my infractions and again I was a failure in my father's eyes.

Returning to Vassar for my sophomore year was again a relief and I was happy to be far away from home. Then my father called, announcing he was coming back for Father's Weekend. I was ambivalent, part of me happy to see him and the other part dreading his visit. While at Vassar, he acted like a single man on the prowl, flirting outrageously with my roommates and spending long hours "meeting" with my advisor, a very attractive woman. Fortunately, all these distractions kept him from commenting on my weight. From Poughkeepsie, he headed down to New York to visit "an old friend," a sophisticated divorcée who (even I knew) had quite a reputation.

By now, even though I longed to cling to the illusion of our perfect family, I had begun to see cracks in the picture. I admitted to myself that my father had flaws. He could be mean and unfair and he had double standards – one for him and another for the rest of the family. The disconnection between his words and actions were becoming more obvious to me. How could he be the devoted, faithful husband he claimed he was when he acted in such suggestive ways with other women? Even with this newfound awareness, his words and personality still overpowered me and I dared not question him about anything.

My beloved older brother Rusty, too, had a powerful influence over me, almost as strong as my father's. We were very close growing up. I worshipped the ground he walked on. Since he was three years older, I was ever seeking his attention. In photographs I was always by his side. As a little girl, when I crossed the street in San Francisco, I reached for his hand. At the ranch, I straddled the log fence that corralled the horses just as he did, climbing to the high rail to sit next to him and I watched him quietly for hours as he carved acorn balls that fell from the live oak tree in our dusty yard. He made cartoon books for me, showing me how to flip the pages quickly to make the drawings move. I laughed, delighted to see his stick figures come to life, running and jumping through my fingers.

The firstborn son, inheriting not only Mom's red hair and lanky frame, but also her sensitive, artistic temperament, Rusty was her favorite child. But he was also Prentis Cobb Hale III and expected to be like his father and follow in his footsteps. Dad tried to mold him into the tough son he wanted him to be and didn't appreciate Rusty's gentle side.

One afternoon when Rusty was nine, he ran into the dining room to show off his new cowboy boots. Not knowing Gee had just waxed the floors, he slipped, fell and started to cry. Frowning, Dad turned around in his chair. "Honestly, Rusty, don't be such a sissy. You don't deserve to wear those boots." As we turned to leave, Dad spied me. "Now HERE'S my cowgirl. Linda, come sit in my lap." At age six, I did so reluctantly, wishing he would say something nice to Rusty. I was unhappy for him and sensed his unhappiness as well.

As soon as I could leave my father's lap, I went to find my brother. He was making something magical out of cardboard. I stood by his side, watching as a roof, then walls and a tiny house burst forth from beneath his able hands. "You can have this," he said, rubbing his eyes hard. I cupped this treasure, carefully putting it on my secret shelf that held all the china animals Frances gave me.

A couple of years later when it was almost dinnertime, Rusty and I, now eleven and eight, were anxiously looking through the *Call Bulletin,* the afternoon paper, in hopes of finding an article interesting enough to talk about during dinner. Dad initiated this program in hopes of improving our conversational skills, insisting we introduce our topic naturally into the flow of talk. At times this was difficult because Mom and Dad talked of people, parties, books, or the opera and Rusty and I were drawn to more dramatic events.

Together we came up with a plan of action. When there was a lull in the conversation, I would casually mention something general about disasters (Rusty had read about a fire downtown). As Gee passed the first course, Hilary got her news in. Then Mom and Dad discussed the merits of Plato vs. Aristotle and we sat up straight, anxiously waiting for a chance to bring up our articles. When Mom paused, I blurted out, "Speaking of Greece, weren't there a lot of fires back then?" Before Dad could respond, Rusty told about the fire in San Francisco that had damaged four buildings. Later he helped me by mentioning cable cars and I told my story about the brakes going out on Hyde Street. I felt great my big brother was beside me, helping me through these ordeals.

At 13 Rusty went to boarding school, leaving me bereft. I wrote him letters, begging him to come home. When he did, I hardly recognized him, he'd grown so tall. Throughout our teenage years we remained close, sharing many of the same friends and going on weekend house parties together. I even fell in love with one of his friends, as he did with one of mine. When he married his first wife, I was a bridesmaid in their wedding and he an usher in my first wedding. When his first son was born, he asked me to be godmother.

Rusty and I, alike in nature, the middle two children, were kindred souls, turning to each other in times of trouble. As my older brother, he technically was "my protector," yet more and more often, I found our roles reversed with my looking out for him instead. When Dad got angry with him, I consoled him, saying I was on his side. Rusty knew how much I loved him, but even so this wasn't enough to counteract Dad's heavy hand and reassure him.

Despite Dad's openly favoring me, which probably planted seeds of resentment in my brother, I never foresaw that Rusty might turn away from me. Nor did I suspect my father would do the same. For far too long, I held the illusion that the two men I most loved while I was growing up would love me in return, because the thought that one day they might not was almost unbearable.

7

Hunting Days

In the summer of 1963, when I was 18, my father took us to Mozambique for a month-long safari. This amazing trip – a milestone in the glory days of the Hale family – would be the last time our entire family would ever travel together. For all of us it would invoke wonderful memories.

In those days most hunters went to Kenya or Tanganyika on safari, choosing the relative safety and reliability of the English outfitters and their covered land rovers. Their guides, called white hunters, were paid professionals, excellent shots who knew where to find game for their clients.

But word had begun to filter out that Mozambique, then a Portuguese-ruled country, was the place to go for true adventure and trophy big game. Wild and virtually untouched by European and American hunters, this beautiful country had few hunting restrictions, abundant wild life and minimal thoughts of game preservation. Rumor had it that the Portuguese white hunters were much more willing to take risks than the English to ensure that their clients had a successful and exciting safari.

Our plane trip seemed interminable, but we were happy in steerage, away from the eagle eye of Dad, in first class with Mom. The boys sat together, with my sister and me across the aisle. She was engrossed in *Uhuru*, the new novel about Africa by Robert Ruark. "Do you really think these white hunters are as handsome and as capable as he describes?" she asked. "No way," I laughed. "He's just romanticizing them to sell books." Finally, we landed in Lourenço Marques (now Maputo), Mozambique's capital.

Climbing down the stairs of the DC-7, we were blasted by the sultry sea air that brushed across the bluest sky I had ever seen. Ahead I saw my parents talking to two men. "Hilary, Linda, come over," Dad called out. "I'd like you to meet Rui and Alberto. They will be two of the white hunters on our trip." As I put out my hand and looked into Rui's dark eyes, framed by jet-black hair, I wondered if in all my years I had ever seen a man as handsome as this one. His crisp khaki shirt was tucked neatly into his safari shorts, showing muscled, brown legs. I could barely mumble hello. On our way to the hotel, my sister threw me a told-you-so look, which, for once, I accepted with good grace.

Since our group was too large for all of us to fit in one bush plane, my father volunteered Rusty to drive with Rui and Alberto the twelve-hour trip into the bush. Our third white hunter, Wally, awaited us at base camp, deep in the wilds. Later Rusty would tell me he wished they had been in a covered land rover, not an open jeep like the one we had at the ranch, because when they had driven through thick brush, large, hairy spiders had dropped from the low hanging branches onto my brother's shoulder. Later, a black mamba, the deadliest and most aggressive snake in Africa, had raced along side their jeep.

When Rui had seen the snake, its shiny, triangular head weaving through the tall grass, he'd sped up, anxious to put some distance between them and the snake. "These snakes can be aggressive if bothered," he had explained to my brother. "And they are fast." Rui had then told a story about a friend who'd spied a black mamba lying across the road. Foolishly he had decided to run over it and as he did, the snake had wrapped itself around the axle. When he'd shifted to increase his speed, the mamba had poked his head through the floorboard and bitten his ankle. In minutes the driver had died.

And so we embarked on an amazing month-long hunting safari in the rugged bush of Mozambique. We were prepared, after much practice, to shoot big game, rifles and shotguns being as ordinary as most anything else in our lives. Growing up I had watched Dad, Rusty and his friends kill deer at the ranch and ducks at their duck clubs and I had followed suit, something Dad expected me to do. Never comfortable with guns, my mother only learned so she could share one of Dad's passions, accompanying him to his duck clubs, on two hunting trips to Africa and one to India. For this trip to Africa, my sister reluctantly joined the practice, with Hap, at age twelve, a more enthusiastic participant.

Leaving the bush plane, we had to cross the Save River to get to our camp. Waiting for our canoe, my mother and I saw sleepy-eyed crocodiles slip noiselessly into the water nearby. As we pushed off from the bank, Wally, our white hunter, said, "Hang on; there is a mother hippo here some-where; you never know when she gets mad." Suddenly the water roiled, rocking our boat and a huge hippo surfaced next to us, her mouth wide open. Wally fired his rifle, miss-ing her; fortunately, she never resurfaced. Our adventures had begun.

Every day driving in open jeeps, we saw wondrous herds of animals: zebra, wildebeest, hartebeest, impala. We ran into groups of eland, cape buffalo, rhino, even the elusive kudu. Prides of lion lazed on the plains, leopard climbed trees to eat the dead impalas we'd shot and hung there and pairs of cheetah raced through tall grass. Wart hogs and baboons abounded, as did dykers and dik-dik – smaller antelopes that stood motionless in the thorn thickets, thinking they were invisible.

Dad divided us into three teams: he and Hap hunted with Rui, Hilary and Rusty were with Alberto and Mom and I with Wally, the oldest, most experienced white hunter. Every morning we awakened at dawn to a cup of steaming tea brought in by a camp boy and then we headed out into the bush, sometimes going all day without seeing the other team, or anyone else for that matter. Dad set up a competition, each team hoping to outshoot the other.

One day, Mom and I were resting by a small pond, wait-ing for the midday heat to subside. After dozing off, I was awakened by the sweetness of water lilies that Wally placed by my side. Suddenly, we heard excited voices of some na-tives who'd materialized out of nowhere to help Wally. They'd spotted a herd of cape buffalo. Jumping into the jeep, we followed them for ten minutes until it was impossible to drive further. Slamming on the brakes, Wally grabbed his rifle in case he needed to back up my mother and off we went into tall grass that at times came up to our chests. We walked as quietly as we could. Stopping short, Wally pointed off to the left where we saw a herd grazing. "Take the one on the outside," he whispered.

Mom shot and the bull lumbered away out of sight. Concerned, Wally conferred with the natives, who told him the buffalo was wounded. Only wielding knives, they took off their shoes, better able, as Wally whispered, to climb a tree should the bull charge. We had heard enough stories around the campfire at night of how smart and dangerous cape buffalo were and how when wounded, they'd often circle back to charge the hunter from behind. I was suddenly aware I was the only one unarmed and that our visibility because of the tall grass surrounding us on all sides was extremely limited. Wally motioned us to stay close to his side.

We heard an angry rustling. "Watch out," he yelled. The grass bent and swayed and a set of heavy, wide black horns swung towards us. The natives ran for the trees. Both Wally and my mother fired and the buffalo fell not forty feet away from where we stood bolted to the ground.

In the ensuing excitement, we forgot about the extremely dangerous situation that Wally had led us into until he said, rather casually, "I say, do me a favor. When we get back to camp, don't mention that we were in such thick grass when we shot that buffalo. I'm afraid I got a bit carried away with trying to outdo the others."

Everyone had adventures. Dad, Hap and Rui, tracking lion, were charged by an angry female that my father had shot and wounded. And then, just days later, Dad invited me to come with them. While Rui and he were off looking for more lion, Hap and I waited in the jeep. We spied a mother rhino with her baby. After eating for a short while, she lifted her head and out of the blue charged right towards us.

Panicking, Hap tried to climb out. Grabbing his shirt, I pulled him back just as she rammed her horn into the side of the jeep. We were unhurt and she walked away. But Hap was so traumatized by the rhino's charge that he spent much of the rest of his time in camp, fishing with Zamba, the cook. At night when the lions roared, he would race to the tent he shared with Rusty to make sure the flimsy flaps were tightly tied, not understanding that with one swipe of a paw, a lion could gain entry into their tent. Fortunately, one never did, although one morning there were huge tracks right beside the tent my sister and I shared.

I think of the young woman I was on that trip, who believed in the safety and goodness of our family and in the integrity of my parents' marriage. Unable to see beneath our façade to problems that were festering, I simply accepted the party line. I couldn't look objectively at myself or my family. At 18 I still struggled to live up to the standards my father set for me, trying to be his perfect, obedient daughter. Feeling the stirrings of rebellion within me, I hadn't yet dared oppose him outright.

During one rest day in camp, I was playing cards with my siblings and the white hunters. Enjoying our respite from the intense hunting competition, we were laughing and being silly. Hap did an imitation of a snorting wart hog. Suddenly, I heard Dad's voice. "Linda, could you come over here right now and sew this button on my shirt for me?"

Without thinking, I made a loud, rude remark. Everyone stopped talking. I prayed Dad hadn't heard me. My heart pounded; I kept looking at my cards, but I felt his approach.

"Young lady," he said in a steely voice, "are you aware of how ungrateful you sound? You get over here right now and do as I say."

"I was just kidding, Dad," I lied. Carefully I put down my cards, our game broke up and I followed him to his tent. I remember this incident as clearly today as when it happened, because it was the first time I voiced aloud any displeasure with him. With one year of college under my belt, I was feeling bolder.

Still, here in the wilds of Africa, as at the ranch, he was more comfortable with himself and his family. He was less frightening and easier to be with. A safari such as this where he could excel with his hunting skills empowered him, making him feel particularly manly and secure. Besides he was always happy when he won. When we sat around the fire at night, drinking vodka and tonics and exchanging stories, comparing our day's shoot and listening to tales the white hunters spun, the rest of us were more relaxed as well. Still, only behind Dad's back did we dare to call him The Pathfinder or Bwana.

On that trip, we saw a number of deadly snakes: Rusty almost stepped on a green mamba, a small, innocuous-looking snake; I shared a shower with what looked like a pile of grey rocks until I realized it was a snake, a puff adder I later learned; and Mom and I saw a spitting cobra slide out from some tall grass and stop, fanning its hoods.

Another day, Wally, Mom and I were searching for a greater kudu, a beautiful antelope that was a prized trophy for big game hunters. My turn to shoot, I rode shotgun next to Wally. Finally, we spotted a buck, blending into the shadows of the forest that surrounded him. My many years of rifle practice at the ranch had served me well and I dropped him with a shot to his neck.

Wally was excited. "You've got yourself a real trophy here," he exclaimed. Back at camp, he held the long, curled horns that measured 55" in length, declaring them eligible for the Rowland Ward Book of Records. Thrilled, Mom and I knew we were winning the family competition. Dad proudly shipped them home and they, along with my mother's cape buffalo horns, hung for many years in our Sugar Bowl home.

I was fascinated with wart hogs, ugly, tough, fearless animals and one day I shot a large male with huge tusks – another trophy, Wally said. When we pulled into camp with the carcass in the back of the jeep, there were visitors, the first and only time we saw white faces other than our own and the white hunters'. To our surprise and delight, we were introduced to Robert Ruark, my sister's favorite author, a stocky, ruddy faced Englishman, also on safari and determined to shoot a record wart hog. Noticing mine, he walked over to inspect the tusks. "Not bad," he said, impressed.

That night we had a magical evening, Ruark adding extra spice and excitement. Hilary brought out her dog-eared copy of *Uhuru*, which he signed, prompting him to tell us about his latest novel, *Honey Badger*, almost finished.

"Why that title?" my father asked him.

Taking a swig of his drink, Ruark answered with words I would never forget because they expressed such a demeaning view of American women. "You know, don't you, that the honey badger is the meanest animal in Africa; it always goes for the balls. My book's really just a critique of American women."

My mother sucked in her breath softly and my father laughed. "Can't wait to read it," he said. Mesmerized by Ruark's gravelly voice and eerie sounds of hyenas shrieking off in the distance, I shivered and drew closer to the fire.

True to form, Dad played practical jokes on everyone, laughing the loudest unless the joke was on him. One afternoon when we were together in camp, he casually asked me to get my sewing kit from my tent. When I opened the tent flaps, a baby wart hog charged me. Startled, I yelled and fell to the ground, as the animal raced off into the bush.

Another day Dad and Rusty leaned a bucket filled with water against a canvas siding of the cook tent, propping it up with the end of a broom. Dad then asked my sister to hold the broom a moment. She did and he exited, leaving her stranded. Realizing she was trapped, my sister, good sport that she was, laughed, finally dropping the handle and completely drenching herself. For the most part, we all enjoyed these pranks.

Eventually, our safari came to an end. For years afterward, I carried with me wonderful, irreplaceable memories of this adventure, a time when our family was happy and still intact. Later, Dad planned other trips, but never again with the entire family. My mother accompanied him to India to shoot tiger; my two brothers went with him to Alaska to hunt for Dahl sheep; and Hap and I went fishing with Mom and Dad in Alaska. The four of us also returned to Africa two years later to bag elephant, the only animal of the big five we hadn't shot.

By the time I was 20, there was a part of me that did not want to kill any more animals, but it was counterbalanced by the father-pleasing part that urged me to perform. And even though I was almost an adult, I was still scared to go against my father. For our second trip to Africa, he bought permits for the four of us to shoot an elephant and of course demanded that I go first. Not strong enough to shoot accurately with a larger caliber rifle, I spent hours (in between sneaking food) practicing with the 30.06 my father gave me. With this smaller rifle, I had to hit the elephant either in his ear hole, or – if he were charging me – in his mouth. Anywhere else the bullets wouldn't penetrate his thick hide enough to kill him.

On that trip we would spend days following and tracking elephant, coming within hundreds of yards of large herds grazing through the trees. I would try to walk as quietly as I could, but being overweight, my thighs would rub against each other, making small swishing sounds that would whisper through the bush. "Shhh," my father would hiss. "You'll scare off the elephants." I would bend my knees to keep my pants' legs from touching. Sweat would pour off my forehead and huge, dark rings under both arms would spread across my khaki shirt. My legs would begin to ache. We would move closer to a herd; then the wind would shift, warning them of our presence and the elephants would fade into the bush, grey shadows swallowed up by the thick brush.

One afternoon we came across a large bull about 150 yards off, standing under the shade of a thorn tree. My hands shook and I could hardly bring my rifle up to my shoulder. Through the scope, the elephant looked much bigger. What if I wounded him and enraged, he charged me? My brain shut down and my body shifted into neutral. Holding my breath, I sighted in on his ear hole and squeezed the trigger. Through my scope I watched this majestic beast slide slowly down on his back haunches. Only when I exhaled did I realize that he was dead.

I turned towards Walter, the white hunter, who clapped me on the back. "Well done," he said.

Squaring my shoulders, I caught my father's eye. "I'm proud of you, Linda," he added. "Not many people can bring down an elephant with a 30.06. And with only one bullet." For that moment I was a "winner," and I basked in the light of my father's approval, relieved and thrilled.

In minutes Africans appeared from nowhere, coming to take all parts of the elephant we didn't want. Back at camp that night, gin and tonic in hand, I retold the story to my mother and younger brother, but I couldn't keep myself from seeing repetitive images of the elephant falling slowly to the ground. I was sad that I had killed this amazing animal and I vowed to myself that I would never shoot a rifle again.

However, a year later my father invited me to accompany him on a kodiac bear hunting expedition in Alaska. Not courageous enough to honor the vow I made in Kenya, I agreed to go. We flew from Anchorage out to the Alaska Peninsula, far from anywhere. Our transportation consisted of two single-engine planes, each flown by an experienced bush pilot. The first day in camp, an unexpected storm blew in and my father and I, along with the two male pilots, huddled inside a small hut, waiting until the weather passed. That day, I wished I were anywhere but in Alaska with three men on a bear hunting expedition, but I was still Dad's girl, willing to do whatever it took to please him.

A few hours later the storm abated and we took off in our respective planes, my father and a pilot in one and I and another pilot in the other. Each plane headed off in a different direction and we quickly lost sight of one another. I held my breath as the plane lifted up and threaded its way through a narrow mountain pass and then flew low again over the stark tundra. All I saw was an endless white punctuated with black rock outcroppings that tumbled down to a distant shore. Looking for any sightings of bear, we skimmed along the gray water and then circled over a low ridge.

Clouds started building up, obscuring my view out the tiny window. The pilot talked quickly into his radio; there was no response. Tossed about by sudden winds, our plane shuddered. We climbed almost to the top of the same pass and then turned back down again, repeating this maneuver for almost an hour before the pilot was finally able to lift our craft high enough to make it over. I had been oblivious to the danger we were in, but as we finally sailed through to the other side, I heard him say "Thank, God." Only then did I realize we had been in terrible trouble.

When we landed at camp, my father was already there, pacing angrily back and forth. "Where in the world have you been? Why didn't you call us on your radio?" he yelled at the pilot. Apologetically, the pilot explained about the unexpected squall and his broken radio. I later learned we had been short on gas as well. Had we been unable to gain enough altitude because of the strong down drafts, we would have crash landed somewhere with no means of contacting anyone for help. After this time on whenever we flew out, my father insisted we keep each other in sight.

On the last day of our expedition, after hours of searching, we finally spotted a bear lumbering down a rocky ridge. Our two planes landed next to each other on a tiny pebbled beach and we climbed out. After checking the direction of the wind, we began to stalk our prey. Secure in the knowledge that this was our last chance to kill a bear, I was relaxed, happy that I wouldn't have to perform. But then, when we came close to where we thought the bear would surface, Dad turned to me. "Linda, I've thought long and hard about who should be the one to shoot; I want you to have this chance of a lifetime." I argued in vain.

Doubts clouded my mind. If I refused to fire my rifle, I was a coward. If I missed, then I would ruin the entire trip and my father's money would be wasted. Plus I would have failed, which was unacceptable in my father's book. At 20 I didn't understand that sometimes it was O.K. to fail. I only knew that Dad loved me when I was a courageous winner and didn't when I was not.

With a heavy heart and even heavier feet, I followed my guide. As we spotted the bear and I readied myself, the wind shifted, warning him of our presence and driving him away from us directly towards my father, who was out of sight. We heard a single shot and then saw my father on the crest of the ridge, beckoning us, signaling thumbs up. Profoundly relieved that I was spared having to perform, I later surmised that an angel must have been there by my side.

In pursuing the bear, we had strayed far from where we landed. It was a long walk back to the planes. Seeing my invincible father struggle with his rifle gave me a glimpse of his less threatening side. Reassured by this display of vulnerability, I offered to carry it for him. He was grateful for my help. Side by side we walked along the edge of the shore, the silvery water lapping quietly up against the rocky sand. From time to time Dad leaned over and patted my arm and I was thrilled by this display of gentleness. We loaded up the planes and headed back to our camp and then Anchorage. On the trip home, my father and I played gin rummy and I beat him every game. For once he didn't mind being the loser. After this Alaskan trip, the last one I took with my father into the wilderness, I ended my rifle-hunting days. I outgrew the need to be Dad's Annie Oakley. Instead, I began channeling my desire to prove myself into pursuits that felt more true to who I was, like writing, tennis and raising a family.

In his growing up years, my father had always looked to nature to ground himself and define his masculinity. As a young man, he had been more comfortable in the outdoors than in the bright lights of city life. But now, at 58 he was changing, gradually leaving his family behind, traveling far from all places wild.

The farther away he wandered, the more lost he became. Eventually he stopped hearing the night owl's hoot and forgot to look heavenward to navigate by the North Star. And then a few years later my mother died from a single shot from one of my father's guns, which until then had been symbols of prowess and success. In one split second, a gun went from being something positive to the instrument that was the catalyst for the ultimate downfall of our family.

8

Biding Time

The night my mother committed suicide, any illusions I still held regarding my parents' happy marriage exploded. No longer could I pretend everything was–or had been–all right. I was 23 and had been married for three short months. Even though I went through the motions of living a normal life, never a day went by that I didn't feel overwhelmed by my mother's death. It was a dark mantle I wore, carrying its heaviness with me everywhere. In my dreams, I felt her sadness and heard her pleas. Unable to run away from my pain, I was forced to face myself.

I entered therapy, first working with Dr. R., a Freudian psychiatrist, the kind, paternal father figure I needed to help me cope. With his steady hand holding mine, I ended my marriage that had lasted only five years. This was incredibly difficult for me to do. I had wonderful in-laws, a loving, kind husband and a beautiful three-year-old son. When I left, I walked away from a family that grounded me with their unconditional love, causing them great unhappiness. Yet I knew that it was not fair to anyone to keep pretending to feel what I didn't feel. Again, just as I had when I'd broken my engagement, I experienced the terribly painful repercussions of not following my heart.

Dr. R. and I often talked of my family and he advised me on how to get along with my father and older brother. But the more I tried to accommodate them, the meaner they acted towards me. I was stuck, drowning in my efforts to appease them. Not until I read Scott Peck's *People of the Lie* and Alice Miller's *Banished Knowledge* did I begin to understand that I was in an abusive situation. These books validated my feelings of injustice, sadness and anger and I looked for another therapist, one who was willing to help me confront the demons of my past.

Ending my therapy with Dr. R. was a difficult move because he had been an emotional mainstay. I began again, this time with a gifted Jungian therapist. With her by my side, I dared to see and feel what had happened to me, thus beginning my process of healing. After months of endless tears, I stopped excusing my father and older brother and let myself see how much they had always tried to control me and still did.

By this time I was remarried to Bill, who was very supportive through these difficult times. Unlike my first husband who disliked confrontation, Bill was willing to take a stand. One of the many reasons I loved him was that he wasn't intimidated by my father; in fact, until I hired a lawyer, Bill was the only voice besides mine that protested aloud when he saw how abusively I was being treated. He was solid, calling a spade a spade, not caring an ounce about what others thought of him, but caring deeply about what was right. As my unswerving advocate, he was refreshingly honest and loyal. Without him I might have lost my way.

Playing tennis, too, grounded me. As a young girl of eleven, I had taken a few lessons but had no friends to play with. I used to practice by hitting an old ball against the uneven stone wall across the street from our house, stopping every few minutes to let a car go by. In my mid-20's, after the birth of my first son, I decided to learn how to really play, not an easy task with no junior coaching or competition under my belt.

Thanks to my father's high standards and his mantra — "Live up to your potential" — I was a high achiever and disciplined. With the help of some wonderful coaches, a talented tennis-playing friend who became my doubles partner and a male friend who was an excellent player, I persevered. In the end, I became good enough to compete and succeed nationally.

From my father I got my competitive spirit, but we used it in different ways. A high stakes kind of guy, he had a fight-to-the-finish, win-at-all costs mentality that raged through him. For me it was always about the effort to excel, to achieve a certain proficiency, to do the best I could. Oddly enough, tennis helped me fight the turbulence in my life, physically centering me on a court with lines and rules. And to succeed entailed practice, discipline and mental toughness, which are all ingredients important to becoming a formidable opponent. I have no doubt that my many tennis competitions prepared me for my upcoming legal battles.

At 26, married with a baby on the way, Rusty was working at a New York investment firm when Dad called to tell him of Mom's death. He struggled, as we all did, to make sense out of what had happened. As the oldest son and already involved in the family financial affairs, he was the most obvious candidate, other than my father, to step in and help take charge. With diplomas from Andover, Yale and Stanford Business School, he had the skills and credentials to be an advocate for us and ensure that we were being treated fairly, more important now with Mom gone and rumors of Dad and Denise's romance clouding the family picture.

Yet Dad still called all the shots and Rusty kept quiet in his father's presence, all the while complaining behind his back about how Dad had manipulated his financial assets after Mom's death to hide much of the community property that was rightfully half our mother's, claiming for his own the bulk of the money, paintings and real estate. He told me that Dad was financially screwing the four of us and that he could prove it with documents he'd seen. Managing to steal a copy of Dad's will, he told me that Dad was not leaving us much money. Believing Rusty, I hoped he would stand up for us. We all knew that my mother would have wanted all of us to get our fair share.

But without her around to diffuse his temper and remind him of his family, my father was visibly changing, more susceptible now to a woman like Denise. She attracted "powerful" men and had much to offer that enticed my father: the glamour of Hollywood, her youthful energy and new, interesting friends who flattered him into believing they liked him for himself rather than for his money and social connections. In return he provided her with financial security and the old guard social credibility she craved.

Until the mid '60s San Francisco society had been made up of old guard San Francisco names – Flood, Haas, Guittard, Folger, Fleishhacker, Sutro, Huntington, Crocker, de Young, Hearst, Spreckels – and unless you were part of the "group" or knew someone VERY WELL who was, it was extremely difficult to break into. Money didn't matter nor did it not get you into places where you didn't "belong".

But by the time Denise became the second Mrs. Prentis Cobb Hale, San Francisco society was changing. New people with lots of money arrived, who donated big sums to the San Francisco Opera, ballet, or symphony and hosted lavish parties. The old guard slowly let down its bar and by the time Denise hit San Francisco, new names and Hollywood names mingled with the staid San Francisco society ones.

When Denise and Dad got married in 1971, two years after my mother's death, they set San Francisco afire. When people read that Hollywood luminaries like Fran and Ray Stark, John Wayne, Doris and Jules Stein, Betsy and Alfred Bloomingdale, Luis Estevez, Ann and Kirk Douglas, Angie Dickinson and Truman Capote (along with his new boyfriend, a gas pumping mechanic) were among the guests at the Hale wedding, they were interested. When they heard that Denise met Gloria Vanderbilt for the FIRST time within a month of the wedding and asked her to be matron of honor, enticing her with such names as Bloomingdale and Capote, they were titillated. But they held back from accepting Denise because they loved my mother. Denise prophetically said, "They might not want me now, but they'll be dying to come to my parties soon."

Years later in the February 1998 issue of *W,* Denise modestly summed up her success as one of the top hostesses in

San Francisco. "When you come to San Francisco today, you have to know me or Ann Getty, just like when you go to Paris, you have to know Alexis de Rede or Drede Mele." In this same article, when she was asked about San Francisco's numerous other hostesses, Denise said, "They're nice people, but where else are you going to go?"

Denise entertained nonstop. A former friend of hers told me how Denise got all these interesting people to attend her parties. "She's very devious," she said. Befriending an important person (X), Denise found out whom he or she admired. Then she called that person (whom she might not even know), inviting him (or her) to a small dinner where she casually mentioned X. would be. With these high profile names, she could then gather interesting guests who wanted to meet Mr. Very Important and Mr. Extremely Interesting. If she were lucky, she got both to attend. If one didn't accept, she'd later explain to the other one that the first had to cancel at the last minute. If both couldn't come, she'd just tell the assembled guests that they'd gotten sick at the last minute. And for a finishing touch she'd add, "I'm so worried about them."

This friend also explained Denise's philosophy. "You must be ruthless when you give a party," Denise once told her. "Only invite interesting people. If wife is boring, only invite husband and if he brings wife, then she's just a piece of furniture that I put with other boring ones."

At these parties Denise would apparently speak so softly —with a heavy accent—that it was very difficult to understand what she said. "I think this is by design," said one guest. "You have to lean towards her to hear what she says, so it looks to the rest of the guests that you're very engaged and that what she's telling you is conspiratorial and important." But he confided that he couldn't hear much and what he did hear was complete nonsense.

She befriended *San Francisco Chronicle* columnist Herb Caen who WAS Mr. San Francisco, Pat Steger, the society columnist and a few key players from the old guard (some people had short memories) and started mixing them with her Hollywood friends. Soon, rarely a day went by that the Hales were not mentioned in one or the other column. Using the same techniques that were so successful for her in Los Angeles, Denise created an "in" group – which she headed and which people soon clamored to be a part of. Hosting many parties, over the years she honored luminaries like Zubin Mehta, Dominick Dunne, Doug Cramer, Angie Dickinson, Don Johnson, Danielle Steel, Georgette Mosbacher, James Beard, Nancy Pelosi, Canadian Prime Minister Mulroney and his wife and Denise's own stepdaughter, Liza Minnelli ("the only stepchild I acknowledge," Denise said).

Early in their relationship, it seemed as if my father had some doubts. H., a close friend of my father's and mine, told me that he'd been asked by my father to do a background check on Denise and tell him what he found out. H. resisted, saying he was extremely unwilling to do what Dad was asking. "If you want to marry Denise," H. said to my father, "marry her. It's your business. But I don't think my gathering of information on her past is a good idea." In the end, Dad insisted.

They met for lunch at the Links Club in New York. I never learned and have no idea what it was that H. told him, but whatever it was, when my father heard, H. said his face turned bright red. They finished lunch, walked out together and shook hands. To my knowledge, Dad never spoke to H. again. A few years later H. saw my father and Denise dining at La Caravelle in New York. He walked right over to their table and said hello, but Dad turned away.

Obviously my father wasn't the only one with concerns. When my mother realized that Dad was seriously involved with Denise, she told Rusty she'd changed her will, now leaving her portion of the estate, including the ranch and her paintings, in particular the Degas, a birthday gift from Dad, to the four children. After her death this will never surfaced. When Rusty asked about it, Dad casually mentioned that it hadn't been properly executed. "Too bad for you kids," he said. "But don't you worry, you'll get it all in the end anyway."

Years later, an acquaintance, M., told me a story about Joyce Haber, a *Los Angeles Times* columnist, who wrote the novel, *The Users* and was a friend of Denise's and my father's. At the time the novel was published, many rumors were circulating that Haber had based one of the characters on Denise.

The story goes as follows: Driving on Sunset Boulevard in a taupe Rolls Royce convertible (top up) to dine at Le Restaurant, M. had as passengers Joyce Haber, Denise and my father. Dad was in the front seat; Joyce and Denise were in the back. Haber mentioned she was working on a "tell-all" book about Hollywood. "It's coming along well," she said to my father and Denise. "I won't use any real names, but of course you know that you're my real heroes."

According to M., my father hit the roof. "Joyce, if you put Denise and me in your book, I will destroy you." They continued on to dinner and although everyone tried to make the rest of the evening fun, it was very stressful. When *The Users* came off the press, my father was furious; calling the *Los Angeles Times,* he threatened to pull all the Carter Hawley Hale ads if they didn't fire Haber. He then bought as many books as he could and destroyed them. He acted as if the story had hit too close to home.

By many accounts, Dad and Denise were happy together, and Dad was willing to give her full access to the family ranch. Before Denise married Dad, we, the four children, had continued to enjoy the ranch, spending much time there with family and friends. After their marriage, she decided she wanted to take over this 10,000-acre spread (the size of almost nine Golden Gate Parks) and suddenly we were ousted from the very place my parents had created for our entire family.

Uprooting us, Denise relentlessly moved in, transforming the simple elegance of the adobe house my parents built into a palatial Hollywood showplace. "This is my labor of love in the middle of nowhere," she explained in a March 1999 *Architectural Digest* magazine article. In her usual tactful way, she said, "... the living room was hideous when I first saw it." Calling the house "little more than a shabby, tacky, neglected adobe lodge," Denise filled it with hand-sewn pillows and tablecloths made from silk imported from Italy. She put silver-framed portraits of male friends such as Cary Grant and Zubin Mehta everywhere and positioned Ming figures, 19th century cloisonné birds, ivory figurines and opulent lacquered commodes throughout the house. In one of the photographs in the article, I saw my record-length kudu horns hanging in prominence in the guest room.

My father and Denise started giving long lunches at the ranch. Invited for 11:30 A.M., those in the know didn't come until one. First-time guests, however, usually arrived a few minutes before noon to find no one was in sight except the butler, who offered Bloody Marys. At one, Prentis, flanked by his two vicious 100-pound German shepherds, Jasmine and Hagen, walked down to the pool to greet his guests. (Those who'd been there before knew to go to the bathroom before Prentis arrived, as any unexpected move set the dogs on edge. The guests had heard that they had twice attacked Rusty; my sister said they almost went after her, too.)

At one such event the wife of the Ambassador to Spain was staying in one of the cottages by the pool, where she had her little dog locked in her room. Jasmine and Hagen kept charging the door, snarling and barking. Guests Milton Friedman and his wife, Rose, both small of stature, were terrified to move from their seats. Thrilled that his dogs were so aggressive and territorial, Dad delighted in watching his guests squirm. At two, Denise, wearing a caftan, finally made her grand entrance. By the time lunch was served one hour later, some guests, suffering from the heat and misjudging how long the cocktail hour would be, were a bit tipsy.

For the ones still sober, the conversation was lively, the food delicious and the surroundings beautiful. Yet I heard a story that reminded me once again of Dad's need to belittle others to prove his worth. At one lunch, he was seated near a gay man. In response to a comment of this guest's, Dad said, laughing, "You're pretty BALLSY, aren't you?" Turning to his seat mate, he added loudly, "I hate those gays."

Thinking he would always be more powerful than she was, hence the person in control, my father underestimated Denise, who ultimately gained absolute power. Immediately, she saw the obvious – that Dad intimidated all four of us and that there was little danger we would band together to confront him (or her) in any way. But she was smart enough to know Dad still needed to be seen as a "family man" and so she patiently bided her time, keeping her distance from family affairs, learning what she could about the dynamics of our family.

But Denise hadn't yet consolidated her power and Rusty had ammunition, enough education and brain power to represent the four children. Instead of stepping up to the plate, however, he chose instead to drop out of mainstream life, moving to Oregon and living a hippie life. After the shock of my mother's death, it seemed clear that he was trying to separate himself from my father and his world. But these efforts were in vain. After a few years, unhappy and yearning for his father's approval, he wrote to my father asking if he could come home to work for him. (If you can't fight them, join them," Dad proudly said in reference to this letter which he showed me.)

The negative repercussions on our family of Rusty first not being brave enough to act in our best interests after Mom died and later aligning himself with Dad and Denise were devastating. For starters, I think, had Dad been initially forced to act accountably to us financially right after Mom's death, Denise would have quickly lost interest.

And had Rusty not teamed up with Dad and Denise, Hilary Farms, a family corporation owned by the four children, would still own valuable properties that would be worth a fortune today. It would be the intact corporation my parents had intended it to be, a way to pass on assets to their children and grandchildren. But Dad was now with Denise, not my mother and Denise had no interest in seeing assets for her stepchildren increase when she had no claim in the corporation. Somehow, my father, after being dedicated for so many years to building up his children's financial assets and investing in real estate, changed his attitude totally.

I clearly remember a Hilary Farms' board meeting where I first dared question one of his business decisions, the precursor to a long battle I would soon wage. Dad was at the head of an immaculately polished rectangular table. I was perched on the edge of a large, upholstered chair on his left with Hilary, Hap and Rusty around the table. Dad's trophy tiger skin lurked in the background. He gave each of us a pile of neatly typed documents. "You don't need to read these," he said. "The information is all there to support why we should sell the real estate."

Since there was no financial necessity whatsoever to sell any of the corporation's real estate holdings and since any moron would realize their potential to appreciate, I spoke up. "Dad," I said, in a shaky voice, "If we sell these properties now, we will never be able to replace them." My face felt flushed and I had a sick feeling in my stomach.

"Linda, that is absurd. Where were you when the brains were handed out? You can invest the money from the sales in the stock market and then buy something else." He immediately insisted on a vote and I was the only one who voted no. Subsequently, Rusty energetically carried out Dad's orders and our six acre piece of lakefront (250 feet) at Lake Tahoe that today would be worth many millions was sold at a bargain price. Other properties followed and soon Hilary Farms was stripped of most of its real estate, its most valuable asset.

My father used to be able to count on my silent acquiescence to get away with whatever he wanted to. But with my sturdy husband by my side, someone who saw how irrational my father and brother were, I was now beginning to be a force to reckon with. The more "rebellious" my paranoid father perceived me to be, the more our relationship deteriorated.

Immediately my father responded to my opposition of his selling off valuable real estate by tightening the screws financially, initiating harsh, unfair policies in my trust. He began billing exorbitant trustee fees that together with other charges offset most of the trust income. Even though my ex-husband stayed on as the third trustee as a favor to me, he had no voice in the management. My father and Rusty set the policy of the trust and had absolute say in the transactions. I began to feel this trust was becoming a vehicle to punish and control me.

Hoping that someday I might be able to counteract their power with some of my own, I decided to start a paper trail. I wrote reasonable letters of protest. Either they didn't respond, their silence and refusal to "see" me sending me down a tunnel of darkness, or they stonewalled, writing formal typed letters, enclosing a copy of the trust document. "We are the trustees in charge and we must remind you that you have no voice in the management of your trust. We are acting in your best interests." When I read these letters, I felt both frustrated with their cold control and ashamed of myself for not being able to do anything to help myself. What happened, I wondered, to that father who professed his love for me and that older brother who once was my friend?

Rusty and Dad, looking for ways to cement their control over me, proposed putting Denise on as a fourth trustee; my father, however, was restricted by the very terms of my irrevocable trust that he, himself, had written that specified only three trustees. Fortunately, he was unable to pursue this course, but I continued to fear their determination to silence me.

Next they proposed Denise as a member of the board of Hilary Farms. I begged my siblings not to let this happen, pointing out the risks of her being involved in this family corporation. They pretended not to understand the repercussions, so when Dad called for a vote, I was again the only dissenting vote. This overtly defiant act further separated me from my family and played right into Denise's hands.

The more involved Denise became in the family financial affairs, the more my father changed. Without the support of my siblings, I alone had little power to balance her growing force or protect what I knew my mother would have wanted me to. And I had no strong legal basis to back up my protests and was powerless against their dictates. Unable to extricate myself from this abusive situation, I walked around with my stomach tied up in knots. All I could do was bide my time and wait for an opportunity to confront them. All I wanted was to hold them accountable to a basic sense of what was right and force them to treat me with kindness and respect.

9

Our Legal Battles Begin

When a thick, legal manuscript arrived in the mail on December 22, 1986, my father, by accident, gave me a rare opportunity and the very vehicle I needed to get his attention. In a cover letter he explained this document was simply a 20-year accounting of my trust and all I needed to do was sign it. Immediately, I was suspicious.

I called a lawyer friend to ask if there were any repercussions in my signing. He told me that by signing it, I would be approving all management decisions made over the past 20 years and relinquishing any recourse to question unfair policies. Both my friend and my husband strongly urged me not to sign until my father addressed some of our concerns about the management of my trust. With this petition, I finally had some leverage and power.

A part of me was scared to challenge Dad; it was much easier to sign the document and avoid any confrontation.

This compliant Linda was the one Dad banked on. But for once he had underestimated me, failing to see the deeper current of emotional strength rising in me, urging me to bear witness for myself.

In challenging my father, I risked forever losing my place in my family. That this could happen terrified me. But I asked myself some hard questions. How long could I tolerate these abusive actions without breaking? Didn't I value myself enough to stand up and ask to be treated fairly and kindly? Didn't I love myself enough to be my own advocate? If I didn't speak up now, even knowing how angry and punitive my father would be, I would forever regret my silence. I might never have another opportunity like this. My husband and I talked for many hours and with his unwavering support and wise advice, I made my decision.

I called my father at the ranch where he and Denise were spending Christmas. I could hardly hold on to the phone, my hand was shaking so much. I heard his loud "Hello" and wanted to hang up. "Dad," I said nervously, "I just received the petition and I have a few questions I'd like you to answer before I sign it." By now I was in a cold sweat.

After an interminable silence, he said, "Just sign it. And afterwards, if you have any questions, I'll answer them."

"No," I said. "No. I need some answers first."

With that he became furious. His words echoed in my ears. "O.K., young lady, if that's the way you're going to play it, fine. Go get your own lawyer." And he hung up.

This phone call left me terribly shaken. Knowing my father's potential for vengeance, I was terrified of the repercussions of my not agreeing to sign the petition. But mixed in with my fear were courageous feelings that came from speaking up in my own defense. For the first time in my life in dealings with my father, I felt empowered.

I didn't sign the petition and a month later in January 1987, my father called me to make an appointment so we could talk. In preparation, my husband and I had carefully reviewed the 70-page accounting of transactions in my trust for the past 20 years. We came up with many questions of how the funds had been used. To my surprise (because Dad had taken all the credit) my trust had paid for my first lavish wedding at the Burlingame Country Club. In addition, funds had also been removed to pay for my sterling silver Irish flatware that had been my major Christmas gift from my father for two years before my wedding.

But we had other more important concerns about the overall management of the trust. We had discovered that as trustees managing my investments, my father and brother had paid no attention to my stock portfolio. With the exception of investing in some of my brother's risky venture capital deals, they had not bought or sold a stock in my trust for over ten years. Here were two men who were knowledgeable about the stock market and investments and were carefully watching and managing their own investments.

In addition, there were no formal trustee meetings even though exorbitant trustee fees were being charged and the expenses of "managing" the trust were all charged to me, the income beneficiary, rather than splitting them with the principal beneficiaries, as was the common practice. After expenses, some months there was little money left to be disbursed as income.

When we entered his office for what we thought was going to be an informal meeting of the three of us, I saw my father seated at his polished desk flanked by two men in business suits. My father introduced them to us as "just friends, lawyers who I think might be interested in your questions." All three men had pursed lips and scowls that darkened their faces.

No attempt was made at small talk. My father stood and I leaned forward to give him a hug. He put out his hand instead. Then we all sat down. I felt rivulets of sweat gathering under my arms. I pressed my knees together to keep them from shaking. My father went right for the jugular.

"Linda," he said, "after all I've done for you, why are you acting in such an ungrateful manner?"

"Dad," I answered in a thin, shaky voice, "I appreciate all that you've given me. I just have some questions about the management of my trust." I paused and silence settled heavily in the room. My words rushed forward. "This isn't about money. I just want to be treated fairly. I just want you to see me as a capable person." After a few questions on trust expenditures that Dad stonewalled, it was obvious that he would not bend. Bill and I stood to go.

"Linda," Dad said, "I'll see you in court."

I don't remember leaving his wood-paneled office or walking past Barbara, his silent secretary, or going down in the plush executive elevator. Bill held my arm and I leaned into his strong body.

Two days later we met with Mr. Dominic Campisi, a respected trust lawyer and explained the situation. We said that our only request was that Rusty, who was now openly (instead of covertly) antagonistic towards me, resign as one of my trustees and be replaced by me or by someone who could act in a capable and unbiased way on my behalf. "It is extremely difficult to remove a trustee," he said slowly, "unless you have some very good reasons."

We explained the history of my trust. When I was 21, I had inherited money from my paternal grandparents. At the time my father had put tremendous pressure on me to sign away these assets into an irrevocable trust, with the income coming to me and the principal going to my children upon my death. He made it clear that I would no longer be welcome in our family if I didn't sign.

To encourage and influence me, Rusty told me he'd signed a similar document when he turned 21. (I later learned this was not the case. Neither sons, only my sister and I, had irrevocable trusts.) The two men I trusted most had presented a compelling case and I had capitulated, signing the document against my better judgment. Only later would I find that I had given up my power to three trustees.

At first, my father, mother and older brother had served as the trustees and when my mother died, my first husband took her place. When we divorced, he stayed on as trustee but was never consulted about the management of the trust. Over the years, this brother and father I trusted started treating me unfairly. I told Mr. Campisi that I had reasonable complaints, such as the high trustee fees and lack of attentive management of the trust.

After Campisi looked over the documents, we met again and he assured me and my husband that we had a good case. No longer under any illusion that Dad was willing to work out our problems without lawyers involved, I was still hopeful that he would be reasonable when he understood that we had valid complaints and that all I was asking for was removal of my brother as a trustee. This way I was not attacking my father or asking him for money, only for a chance to be treated more fairly.

Now armed with a representative from his world of power, I naively believed my father would listen to me. But as I entered his office and saw two lawyers from an elite and powerful San Francisco law firm at his side, I remembered overhearing words my father said angrily once to someone on the phone: "Ed, never, never cross a Hale man." He was ready for battle, not negotiation.

Stonewalling any of our requests for documents, he and his lawyers also stated unequivocally that Rusty would never resign as trustee of my trust. I was angry and hurt that Dad gave my older brother credibility as he dismissed me and my ability to serve just as capably as a trustee, which was permissible by law.

"Your father's a tough one," Campisi said, as we were going down in the elevator. "He wants to throw your husband down a cinnabar mine. And his lawyer took me aside before we left and said, 'Mr. Campisi, if you want to get into litigation, just know that we'll feed you and your client all the barbed wire we can.'"

When Mr. Campisi repeated these mean-spirited and confrontational words to me, I knew we were at war and that my father and his lawyers would be as vindictive as they possibly could. (And they were.) I was shocked at the cruelty of those words and consumed with dread, but I couldn't let myself absorb their power or I might have given up right then.

By challenging my father in this way, I was inadvertently cutting the last remaining threads of our relationship, making it impossible for us to have one in the future. He hated to lose and always fought – with his take-no-prisoners' attitude – to the finish. With his vast connections, deep pockets and determination to crush any foe, even his once "favorite" daughter, he was a formidable opponent.

Our legal battle quickly escalated into full-out war. Through the grapevine from a friend in the investment business, I heard he told my siblings that he would spare no expense with legal fees, just as long as he "brought me to my knees." I suspected Denise was thrilled I was finally the family pariah, the person everyone else in the family could blame for all the troubles. Gathering my brothers and sister to her and my father's side, she and Dad made it clear to them that they were to have nothing further to do with me or my children, initiating a scorched-earth policy that destroyed all bridges of family support.

I still held out hope that my sister, who had the same trust as I did and stood to benefit from all my protests, wouldn't desert me. Her 50th birthday was coming up. I heard from friends that she was giving herself a large party. When my invitation never arrived, I called Hilary, still hanging on to the threads of our relationship.

"Hil, aren't Bill and I invited to your party?" I began.

She was flustered. "No, you're not." I started to cry.

"Don't you understand my position?" I asked her. "This will be just one more public statement reinforcing my exile from the family."

"I'm sorry," she said. "I just can't include you."

Years later, she told me what had led up to her decision. Gathering her courage, she had called Dad to tell him she was giving herself this party and that she intended to invite everyone in the family. This was her small way, she hoped, of trying to bring us all together. "Hilary," Dad said. "If you invite Linda and Bill, Denise and I won't come and I'll make sure the boys and their wives don't come either."

After their conversation ended, Hilary sat outside on the steps of the Burlingame Country Club and sobbed. With a heavy heart, she went ahead with the party. The day after her party, she told me, Dad called to say what a huge success it had been. "When are you going to have another one?" he asked. Not for a long time, my sister said to herself, realizing how hurtful and manipulative my father had been.

By this point, many people knew of our family struggles. I could no longer pretend I was part of a happy family. However, until this night when my sister told me I wasn't invited to her party, I hadn't let myself quite believe that my family had totally turned against me. I was still wearing a protective armor of illusion to blunt the pain. However uneven and meager my family's support had been in the recent years, I still counted on them emotionally. Now that I realized all ties had been severed, I was devastated.

I leaned on two men in my life who were my champions. My husband never stopped believing in the rightness of my cause. His strong dislike for my father, his practical, straightforward approach to our legal problems, his toughness and his outrage at how my family was treating me helped me cope. Beyond that, my brilliant, fair-minded lawyer, Dominic Campisi, never lost sight of what I wanted. He knew that for me this battle was never about financial gain or even financial autonomy. It was about asking my father and brother for fair treatment and asking my other siblings to stop condoning abusive behavior in our family.

Why did I embark on this journey when I knew from the

start that the financial and emotional costs would be tremendous? The reasons ran deep below the surface of my life. After years of being treated badly by my father and older brother, I finally decided I couldn't live with myself any longer. I remembered back to that beloved little girl of six and wanted to honor her. I heard a voice inside me saying I would no longer put up with their abusive behavior and I would not give in as my mother did.

After months of posturing and delays, we were finally able to set a date to depose my older brother. As one of the three trustees of my trust, we wanted him to answer our concerns about the management. When I walked into the law firm of Brobeck, Phleger for the deposition, I saw my two brothers, my father and two of their lawyers seated on the far side of a long, polished mahogany table. They were a mass of pin-striped blue suits and brown leather briefcases that snapped, snapped, open and shut. Near them at the end sat the court reporter. Mr. Campisi, my husband and I positioned ourselves opposite them. They continued talking and never once looked our way; for their purposes I was invisible. I was the only woman in a room of eight men.

Locked in combat with members of my family, here I was in the conference room of a prominent law firm, living my worst nightmare. I squared my shoulders and looked across at my family. It was hard for me to believe that we were at war over this simple situation, one so easily resolved if my brother would only resign as trustee.

Aside from his incapable management of my trust, many times he had demonstrated hostile behavior towards me, not a quality one wants in a trustee. My then sister-in-law later told me she had wanted to reach out to me during this time, but Rusty had forbidden her to do so, saying, "So you'd let a rattlesnake come to your front door?"

If Rusty resigned, my father and ex-husband could replace him with me or agree on another trustee, one who would certainly be more fair-minded than my brother. I was grateful for this opportunity to set the record straight. Armed with my lawyer, I hoped they would finally listen to me and be forced to acknowledge that my brother, at least, was too emotionally biased to look out for my best interests.

Together I thought we could come up with a fair solution. But early into my older brother's deposition, I lost hope. After Rusty repeatedly answered "I don't recall" or "I have no knowledge of that" to many questions, I felt completely discouraged because clearly there was information I had hoped he would know. In Hap's subsequent deposition, he followed Rusty's example and also had great difficulty remembering anything. When the questioning was over, my father shook hands with my lawyer and walked out with my brothers and their lawyers. Not once did they look my way. I felt empty and heavy-hearted as I looked at their disappearing backs.

A few months later, when I deposed my father, we met in his lawyers' offices. My hands were cold and I kept them tightly clasped together under the table. Here I sat, across from my very smart Stanford Law School-graduate father, aggressively challenging him in the very power world he dominated. I kept my eyes steady on his face, yet he tried never to look at me.

Once when he was being particularly evasive, I caught his eye. He was rattled. "Can you get my daughter to stop looking at me?" he asked my lawyer. At the break he went over to Mr. Campisi. "I want you to tell Linda," he said, "that if she continues on with all this, I will disinherit her children, too."

"Is that a threat?" my lawyer asked, laughing. His kind, jovial manner helped diffuse the darkness that enveloped the room. When Mr. Campisi later told me what my father had said about disinheriting my children as well, I was shaken. He'd hit me where it hurt the most. Because of my decisions and actions, my children might bear the repercussions of his vengeance.

I was next in the order of depositions. During preparation I had asked Mr. Campisi for advice. "Linda, you'll do just fine," he said. "You've gone over all the documents; just tell the truth. That's all you have to do. Oh and only answer one question at a time." I dreaded the prospect of having to sit across from my father again. But when I entered the conference room, only my two brothers and their two lawyers were there. The same court reporter sat at the end. My father was gone.

Having been told the deposition should last only a day, I steeled myself for their endless questions, for the details and numbers I must remember, for the traps they would set, the intimidation tactics they would use. Flanked by my husband and lawyer, I sat across from my brothers. I took a deep breath that calmed my wildly beating heart. Raising my hand, I swore to tell the truth and nothing but the truth. I then stated my name and address. There was no turning back now. Focusing totally on the task at hand, (just as I did when I played a national tennis tournament), I turned off my emotions and competed, ironically, something I had been raised to do. When they tried to confuse me, I requested they clarify their questions and when they asked me a compound question, I reminded them to ask only one question at a time. Never did they trip me up.

They bombarded me with unnecessary questions that had nothing to do with the real issue but that demanded knowledgeable responses. They hoped to wear me out. As the first day ended, my lawyer took me aside. "It's obvious they want to prolong this deposition for as long as they can," he said. "There's nothing we can do except coöperate." He conversed with the opposition and then informed me there would be at least two more days of depositions. "You're doing great," he said by way of encouragement.

I knew that if I let myself feel any of the pain and sadness that came from being interrogated by lawyers representing my family, I would stumble and probably falter. Determined to persevere and win, I kept these emotions sealed away, thinking only about their questions and my answers.

After three long days it was over. I knew I had told the truth and hopefully hadn't helped their case in any way. Campisi praised me. "You're tough," he said. "They met their match with you, mark my words." He continued, "You know, Linda, you are one of the three best witnesses I've ever had. You answered their questions precisely, you never got rattled. I remember saying to myself 'man, she is really good'." His kind and complimentary words, though bittersweet to my ears, touched my heart.

A few days later an excited Campisi called me. "Linda, your brother has resigned as trustee and your father agrees to replace him with you." Unable to fully believe that I had achieved my goal, I was speechless. When his words finally sunk in, I felt all at once relieved, exhausted, worn down emotionally and happy the ordeal was finally over. I also felt vindicated.

But our moment of triumph was short lived. Knowing now that my ex-husband, who took a dim view of how my trust had been handled and I, as the new trustee, could out-vote him, my father, now in the minority position, resigned as trustee. He then outfoxed us. He invited Campisi and me to a meeting of Hilary Farms Corporation, the family corporation owned by the four children and the major asset of my trust. When we entered his office, the rest of the family, including Denise, was already assembled. As a new lawyer handed us a thick document, it became readily apparent that everyone except for Campisi and me knew of its contents.

Without our knowledge, my father had orchestrated a plan wherein Hilary Farms, our family corporation of which my trust owned 25% of the stock, was to be changed from a corporation to a limited partnership, with Dad becoming general partner. With Hilary Farms as a corporation, my trust had voted 25% of the stock. As part of this newly formed limited partnership with my father as the general partner, I was rendered powerless. In this new position my father had full authority to do whatever he wanted. This action was his answer to his resignation and loss of control over my trust.

Clearly, my father made this change from Hilary Farms being a corporation to becoming a limited partnership to keep me from having any say whatsoever in the workings of Hilary Farms. This move showed how determined he was to silence me and cost everyone, excluding my father, hundreds of thousands of dollars, ultimately causing the destruction of Hilary Farms.

As my lawyer flipped through the document, he was grim. "This is 40 pages long. We need to read this before Linda will agree to anything," he said.

Denise interrupted, "There's no time for that. We vote right now." Dismissing Campisi's protests, my father, Denise and my siblings voted yes.

Outvoted and outraged, my normally unflappable lawyer stood up and we left. "There is no way they can ambush you like this," he fumed. "Talk about Draconian measures. They have once again violated their fiduciary duties by not giving you a chance to protect your rights." Just when I thought I was finally in control of my own affairs, just when I hoped my father might treat me as a mature human being, he pulled this fast one on me.

After that meeting Campisi felt, as I did, that we had no choice but to oppose their actions. We knew my father, once again in a position of power over me, would be more vindictive than ever. Both my father and older brother held grudges and given their previous actions, there was no chance of my being treated fairly. Discouraged to have lost much of the ground I had gained in the first negotiations, I was tired of fighting. And legal fees were rapidly shrinking my bank account.

I knew, however, that I could not stop now. After all we had just experienced, I must fight to the finish. To pay more legal bills would strap me financially, but other than that, what more could I lose that I hadn't already lost? Besides I had much to gain—namely freedom from ever having to be in a subservient position to my father or brother again. Then, maybe, I could piece my soul back together.

By now it was September 1988. Because there were valuable real estate assets in Hilary Farms and because I now had no voice in the operations, Mr. Campisi decided that it was in my best interests to partition out my 25%of the assets in any way we could all agree upon. Over the intervening months, he offered many alternatives, all of them fair to the four owners – my two brothers, sister and me. All my siblings had to do was vote "yes", but my father couldn't stand to set me free and they did not dare overrule him.

By not acting in their best interests and mine, they prolonged the lawsuit for three more years, allowing Dad to spend much of the corporation's money. (He told them not to worry about any of the legal costs, assuring them he would finance whatever it took to crush me, a promise he later reneged on.)

To the ultimate detriment of all four of us, my siblings stood with my vindictive and irrational father, never finding the courage within to confront him and demand he pursue a fair and reasonable course. In December, 1991, I opened a letter informing me that a court date was set for January, 1992. Knowing too well that my father would never settle and was determined to see our battle through to the end, I was anxious and nervous about our January court confrontation.

One afternoon in mid-December, my lawyer called to tell me he'd heard my father had a stroke. "He can't talk," Campisi said. Having access to no further information about my father's condition but knowing that for the moment he was incapacitated, I was relieved, profoundly relieved. With his "take-no-prisoners and crush-her-no-matter-what-the-cost" voice momentarily silenced, I saw a chance for my siblings and me to agree. Sure enough, when my father was not there to speak for my brothers and sister, they settled with me on the courthouse steps. Overall, I was happy to have this ordeal over, but I was also angry and disappointed that my siblings hadn't found the courage to work this out years before.

Ironically, with my father silenced, I finally achieved what I had wanted for so long – financial separation from my family. At no time during our five years of protracted legal battles did I ask for money. For me the struggle had been about principles and relationships. My only goals had been to replace my older brother as trustee of my trust with anyone who would be capable and fair and then after Dad's end run, to separate out my one-quarter interest in the limited partnership.

But for my father this had been only about money and power. In asserting my personal strength, I had committed the ultimate act of betrayal in his mind, one he would never forgive. With hundreds of thousands of dollars spent on both sides over a long five year period, our war was over. Cut loose from the perverse control of my father and older brother, I was free to make my own decisions.

10

Saying Good-bye to My Father

My anger spent, played out through endless depositions and court appearances, I was left with a deep sadness. Grateful that our family was spared further legal traumas, now I was worried about my father's health.

I had no idea how sick he was and because I was the family pariah, none of my siblings (or anyone else who might know) dared call me to tell me what was going on. I couldn't find out any reliable details and waited anxiously, hoping to hear some good news of his recovery. One day my husband bumped into Jim, an old friend, who asked him if he was going to The Wedding. "What wedding?" Bill asked. "Your father-in-law's," Jim responded. "Everyone is going."

Surprised that Dad was recovered enough to go out, I wondered why he and Denise were renewing their marriage vows 21 years after they had first wed. We heard nothing about the ceremony until an acquaintance who attended the wedding – perhaps he knew how starved I was for any details of my father's condition – gave us a video he took of the service. He told us that the ceremony took place in a Serbian church high up on a hill in San Francisco. When my husband and I sat down to view the video, we grew so uncomfortable that we found it difficult to watch. We were incredulous. How could the 100 or so assembled guests, including my siblings, possibly have watched Denise put my obviously ill father through this bizarre ceremony?

According to bystanders and from the video, Rusty wheeled Dad to the altar. There he sat, unmoving in his wheelchair. Then conductor Zubin Mehta walked Denise, dressed to the nines, down the aisle. In the video I noticed that my father was slouched over and his mouth was slightly open. He looked so different from the strong, capable man I last saw in his deposition. It must have been a Serbian custom, with Rusty, the Best Man, dancing around Dad and then placing a wreath upon Denise's head. With the bride and groom nearby, the Serbian priest, decked out in his finest robes, waved incense. My sister told me most of the liturgy was sung and that she didn't understand a word.

The camera then panned to the pews, filled with familiar socialite faces – Ingrid and Ruben Hills of Hills Bros. Coffee, Ann and Gordon Getty and Carmella Skaggs, Boz' ex, all looking supportive and sincere. After the service everyone moved over to a lavishly decorated hall, where a massive wedding cake, similar to the one Elizabeth Taylor had at her most recent wedding, was the centerpiece attraction. (We were told it was flown up from Hollywood for this special occasion.)

My sister admitted later that Dad looked very weak.

When she went up to him after the service, she doesn't remember his saying a word to her. Years later, my then sister-in-law told me that "Your poor father was hardly alive. He was so sick and obviously shouldn't have been out of the hospital. It seemed so mean. The only reason I could see for Denise putting him through all that was her concern that he might die and she wanted to be sure she was legally married."

I wondered why Denise chose to expose Dad publicly when he was at his most vulnerable state. The father I knew hated to ever show any weakness and surely Denise must have known this as well. Rather, he prided himself on powering his way through any situation. Denise explained (to my sister and others) it was because she had promised her mother that before her mother died, she would be married in the church. Whatever the reasons, after the cake was cut, my brother wheeled my father into a van that drove them back to the convalescent home.

After much deliberation, weeks after the wedding, I gathered my courage and decided to visit him. Now that he was weaker and more vulnerable, I hoped he might forgive me. Scared that he wouldn't, I forced myself to walk up the narrow, carpeted stairs to the second floor of the hospital. I started to shake. At the reception desk, I asked a nurse if Mr. Hale was seeing visitors. "Yes, he is," she said.

"How is he doing?" I asked.

She was friendly, open. "He's tough; he's doing a little better. Come, follow me."

"Wait," I said. Because I was the outcast and Hilary was still in favor, I needed to make clear which daughter I was. "Tell him first it's his daughter Linda who is here." She gave me a puzzled look, but then walked to the far end of the room where my father lay motionless. From where I was standing, a distance away, I saw that his legs were bent and he was wearing brand new jogging shoes, tied neatly in matching white bows. By his side a therapist held a large orange ball and guided his right arm, up and back, up and back. Hypnotized by this simple motion, I stood still, as if I, too, were paralyzed. Off to the side, I saw Denise, her Slavic profile caught by the flickering lights of the T.V. I hovered behind the doorway where Denise couldn't see me. Returning, the nurse couldn't look me in the eye. "I'm sorry," she said, "but now is not a good time for a visit. Maybe another day would be better."

Knowing there might not ever be another day, I lost it, tears tumbling down my cheeks. I remembered I had a picture with me of my three boys and so I gave it to the nurse. "Please," I said, "make sure he sees it." "I promise," she said.

That night Hap, who hadn't spoken to me in over six years, called me on the phone. "I must see you right away," he said. I recognized the hurried flatness in his voice.

"Just tell me now," I answered, already knowing what he would say. "Get it over with."

"No," he insisted. "I am to see you in person to make sure there is no misunderstanding."

He drove from his home in the redwoods, and then he, Bill and I sat around our kitchen table. I offered him tea, coffee, cookies and fruit, but he declined. Our meeting lasted no longer than two minutes. In his sternest and most authoritative voice he said, "Denise wants you to know that if you ever try to see Dad or talk to him again, she will get a restraining order out against you."

Even though his words didn't take me by surprise, the

fact that he, my little brother, my mother's son, agreed to carry any message for Denise, much less one as hurtful as this one, still rocked me deeply. I had to believe that it was painful for him as well to carry out this horrible mission for Denise. After Hap left, my husband took me in his arms and held me there for a long time.

Over the next months, I began to hear from various people that Dad was making a remarkable recovery. When my husband and I attended the funeral of a close friend's father, I saw firsthand that he could now walk. Already seated, I watched as he and Denise walked slowly down the aisle and sat across from us. I was scared all over again. When the service was over, I gathered my nerve and approached him. "Hello," I said.

"Hello," he answered, looking over my head.

I started nervously filling the air with words, but he didn't respond. Finally I asked, "Dad, aren't you going to talk to me?"

"I've already said hello," he said, his face a mask as he limped away.

A year later, I saw him downtown on Powell Street. Still intimidated, part of me wanted to just watch him walk on by, but then I willed myself to go over to him.

I touched his arm. "Dad," I choked. "Dad."

Turning to me, he fixed his narrow, dark eyes on mine. "Linda, I have nothing more to say to you – ever again." And he was off, threading his way unsteadily through the crowd. My throat closed up; I felt like suffocating. I wanted to call out "I love you, Dad," but the words wouldn't come out. I would not see him again until he was unconscious and dying in the hospital.

One Sunday I was attending services at Grace Cathedral. A fellow trustee of the cathedral, S., a doctor I didn't know well but who was a good friend of my stepmother's, approached me. Knowing that Dad and I were estranged, S. told me Dad was in the hospital. "It looks serious," he said. "If you'd like to write him a note," he added, "I will bring it to him for you." At that moment we were cohorts. Should my stepmother, the keeper of the gate, have found out that he had smuggled in anything from me, she would have been furious.

I began a short note to my father. "Dear Dad," I wrote. "I hope you know that I love you very much and that I am always by your side. If you want me to come see you, I will be there in an instant." Then I gave this note with some lilies of the valley to S., who called later to say he personally delivered them to Dad. "He seemed happy to receive them," S. reported. Although I never heard from my father or anyone else in the family, I was forever grateful to this man for giving me this small sense that I touched my father before he died.

When it became clear that Dad was dying, my older brother told me, Denise huddled with her lawyers. She cautioned him, "Remember, Rusty, if anyone tries to make will change in hospital, grounds for lawsuit." When my sister's son, Tommy, came to visit Dad in the hospital, Denise said to a friend, "What's he doing here? Tommy, he's a BIG loser." And to my sister she said, "I'm NEVER letting Linda in here to see your father."

Despite his weakened state, according to my older brother, my father begged to be taken home. He wanted to be surrounded by his beautiful paintings and hear his beloved operas once again before he died. But Denise was adamant that he stay in the hospital. "You don't understand," she said to Rusty. "If he goes home, people who take care of him steal things like ashtrays. This happened to very good friends of mine."

Dad died about ten on a Friday morning. My younger brother and his wife were away on a trip, but Rusty and his son, Prentis IV and Hilary and her son Tommy were by his side. The ultimate night owl, Denise, was asleep in their luxurious apartment, surrounded by her ashtrays and antiques and didn't arrive until later that day.

After Dad's death I learned from my brothers that Dad had, in fact, wanted to see me, but that Denise had been determined to keep me away from him, no matter what. Hap told me she did not want me to know he was dying and commanded, "Do not tell Linda where your father is or what bad shape he is in." And Rusty said she was enraged that I'd managed to communicate my love to my father through the note that S. had smuggled in for me. "Why is Linda sending your father this note?" she yelled at Rusty. "Is she trying to get back in will or what?"

The night I sent the note to my father, I dreamed that I was with an older man who had white, tufted hair and a kind smile. He was flying a plane and I was the passenger. We flew low over the family ranch and Sulphur Creek, snaking our way between steep canyon walls that eventually opened up to the gravel bar that stretched out in front of the little house at the ranch. Somehow I realized this was his last trip, that he was going to die and so I reached out my arms and hugged him. I was crying, yet I felt that he was accepting his journey and happy that I was with him. Suddenly I understood that the pilot was my father and that he was taking me back to the ranch, the place where he loved me and the rest of the family in the best of ways. When I woke up, my cheeks were wet; I knew my father would die soon.

A week later the phone rang; it was Denise. Her voice was matter-of-fact. "Linda, your father made me promise not to let you visit him, but now that he is unconscious, you may go to the hospital." I was off in an instant to be by his side. When I entered his room, my feelings were suspended, my heart and body detached. I understood though that the reconciliation I had dreamed about earlier would now never come to pass.

Dad looked so helpless lying there, his arms mottled deep purple, his paper-thin skin bruised from age and the tubes attached to a body that no longer moved. Emotionally bankrupted by the choices he had made in his life, he seemed so frail and lonely, unable to hear my voice of love, unwilling to access the landscape of his heart. Stroking his smooth forehead, I took his hand in mine. I was no longer afraid.

A nurse hovered around his bed. I asked her for some time alone and she left. Sitting there, holding a hand that couldn't feel my hand, looking into eyes that couldn't see me, I felt this sadness deep inside that stayed there, heavy, as unmoving as my father. Minutes ticked by. Hoping beyond hope that he might hear me, I started talking to him, telling him all the things I wished I'd been able to say before.

I told him all about my life, about how I wished he could have shared in some of my triumphs and failures, how I yearned to feel safe enough to lean my head against his shoulder and feel his arms around me. I told him that all I wanted was for him to see me, hear me and treat me fairly. I explained that his sharp tongue, his willfulness, his need to control and bully me almost put me over the edge and that I had to fight back or I might have died just like Mom. I admitted that I had been terrified to stand up to him.

Then I began recalling all the good times, especially at the ranch, when the air was still and heavy with jasmine and we sat together outside under a blanket of stars. I'm glad, I added, that he always picked me to be on his team when we played "Hare and Hounds" because I got to ride next to him and choose where to tie the next ribbon. (And because we always won.) "Do you remember the day," I asked him, "when we were out in the jeep looking for deer and I saw a huge buck far off and you, patting me on the knee, said I had the keenest eyes of anyone? And the time in Alaska when we were bear hunting, lost and miles from the plane and I carried your gun and mine?"

Finally, I told him that I loved him. And I thanked him for life and all the wonderful gifts and opportunities he'd given me. Before I left, I remembered to mention that I have hanging in my study three pictures of him as a baby sitting in his father's lap. In the picture, his left hand is clasping his father's wrist and he is smiling and looking up adoringly at his father, my grandfather, with love and absolute trust. Later, alone in my study, I would close my eyes and pretend that I was that baby being held by my father, imagining that he was looking down at me with love. I could almost see him smile.

When I left my father that Friday morning, I knew I wouldn't see him again. Sure enough, around noon that day, February 16, 1996, Rusty left a message on my machine saying Dad had just died. When I heard this, I sat in silence, wondering if Dad and I would ever meet again. If we did, next time I would be less afraid to speak of love and maybe, just maybe he wouldn't be afraid to answer. Perhaps I would walk towards him and perhaps he would open up his arms wide, pulling me in close to his heart.

Years later I had lunch with an older cousin, who had stayed in touch with my father until his death. We filled each other in on what was happening in our lives. I told him I devoted much of my time to my family, as a wife to Bill and mother to my sons. I was actively involved in their schools, serving on numerous committees and raising money. In whatever time was left, I wrote and competed in tennis.

We talked about my troubled relationship with my father and how I wished it had been different. Sensing a slight disapproval on his part, stemming from his not really understanding why I had to fight my father, I asked if he had any insights into my behavior, any thoughts on how I could have handled the situation better.

"You know, Linda," he said slowly, "your father once told me what high hopes he had for you and how disappointed he was in how you turned out." The Linda of years ago would have been decimated by his remarks. But after all I'd been through, of course they still hurt, but I was coming to understand that my father, not I, had been the disappointment. He had simply been too scared of facing himself to ever see me for myself.

11

Berthe Morisot

Even though Dad and I were estranged at the time of his death, I had never given up hope that we might reconcile. The realization that this would never happen hit me hard. Fully expecting my siblings and their children to be remembered in Dad's will, I prepared myself for the loneliness I knew I would feel upon being the only one punished after his death, as I had been when he was alive. When I heard that he cut them out of his will as well, leaving his entire estate including our beloved ranch, with no strings attached, to Denise, I was stunned. Why, I wondered, had my father treated us and his other grandchildren all in the same callous way?

After all, my siblings toed the line for many years, either actively supporting my father and Denise in their power hungry ways or passively condoning them by never daring to speak up against any of the destructive and divisive actions that tore our family apart. They didn't give Dad any reason to disinherit them. Many might see the obvious and figure that at the end of his life, he was so under the control of his wife he totally capitulated to her demands that she get everything. That was the most likely scenario.

But there was another possibility that helped me rationalize my father's actions. Maybe I wasn't singled out for punishment because on a certain unconscious level he admired me for being the only one to stand up to him. In a funny way, because I fought him tooth and nail, I remained his daughter to the end.

While I felt bad for my siblings and their children, being on the same level playing field, for once, made it easier for me. I felt less alone. Now I even dared hope that we might be able to be friends again, since this time power and money would not get in the way. And I was profoundly relieved none of us had to be connected any longer to Denise. "So the story is ended," I said to my husband. "She got what she wanted."

About a month after my father's death, Denise (whom I hadn't heard from for years except for that one mean call telling me Dad was unconscious) phoned to say her chauffeur was dropping off some family pictures and some letters. She then mentioned that I was always Dad's favorite and that she had almost convinced Dad to reconcile with me, which was why she said I could go to the hospital to see him when he was in a coma. I was shocked at her transparency, knowing full well that she had never tried to unite our family when Dad was alive. She said she wanted to have lunch with me to talk and get things straight. And in ambiguous and threatening terms, she warned me about Rusty. "I watched when he came crawling back in; I watched him do more damage than anyone I've known. We will have a war."

Now I felt very uncomfortable. Even though I had no relationship with my siblings, I was still more loyal to them than I was to Denise and the last thing I wanted was to be involved again with anyone who, I felt, based many of her relationships on money and power. A few days later she called again, this time to invite my three sons up to the ranch – without Bill or me – for the day. I was extremely conflicted. Because I had stood up to my father, I was responsible for his disowning my sons. If I didn't go along with Denise, did I ruin their chances of inheriting some of his money from her? I decided to let them go. Ironically enough, the day that worked for everyone was July 30, which would have been my father's 86th birthday.

After their visit, Denise informed me that my sons were now in her will. She said that when she got to know them better, she would "improve their chances". "Christian is adorable," she said. "And John is original and I like people who are that way. He is not a sheep. He has a great personality and is very handsome." I felt as if I were being sucked right back into a place from which it had taken me years to escape.

But did I have the right to deny my children a chance of having a relationship with Denise? Perhaps, I argued to myself, however unconvincingly, we could begin anew; perhaps Denise would play fair, now that Dad was dead. But I had a sinking feeling that I was fooling myself and that nothing had changed. There was just one fewer player now. And I wondered why she was being so nice; what did she want from me? It didn't take long for me to find out why.

Soon thereafter my older brother Rusty called. Other than his message on my machine telling me of Dad's death, I hadn't heard from him in 15 years. He said that in going through some files of the family's art work, he found, to his surprise, sales agreements for two Impressionist paintings showing that they were bought in our names and paid for from monies taken from the four children's accounts. It appeared that Dad and Denise had sold one, an Alfred Sisley, in 1978 and kept the funds, but the other one, a Berthe Morisot, currently hung in Denise's living room.

I was surprised about the Sisley ownership, but not about the Morisot, because years ago, when our parents told us we children owned it, we had often joked about dividing it into four pieces. During my legal battles with my father and older brother, my lawyer asked many times in depositions about this painting, hoping to find records proving that I owned one quarter, but both Dad and Rusty denied the painting was owned by the four children. When Rusty told me he had already filed a claim for the paintings and for other assets of my father's, I began to understand why Denise was making overtures to me.

I talked with my younger brother and older sister, trying to figure out whether or not we should follow suit with our own claim. We knew we were the rightful owners and that principle was at stake here, but we were not sure we had enough proof. Aside from wanting justice to be done, we had an emotional claim here, too. Before it was in my father and Denise's living room, this beautiful Impressionist painting used to be the centerpiece in our Broadway Street living room where we grew up, a lovely reminder of the time when we were a family together.

Entitled *En Bateau sur Le Lac de Boulogne,* it is a painting of Milly, Morisot's favorite model and Julie Manet, the artist's daughter, who are feeding swans on the lake in the Bois de Boulogne. A beautiful painting, it is vibrant with blues of the lake and the clear, startling white of the three swans swimming towards the boat.

Hilary, Hap, Bill and I met at our house. We were polite and formal with each other, treading lightly in this newfound connection. After we looked over the well-documented business records, including ledgers that showed all the transactions, we saw that the evidence was overwhelmingly in our favor and decided to go ahead with a plan to repossess our painting. We agreed to hire Mr. Campisi, the very lawyer who had represented me against them in the last lawsuit.

Since Denise had reëstablished contact with me, as a courtesy, I called to tell her we had airtight documents proving our ownership of the painting. Explaining that we needed to have our lawyer file a claim before the statute of limitations ran out, I asked if she would return it to us to avoid any further legal conflicts.

This was a hard first test of our tenuous new relationship; I wondered if she would be reasonable and fair. After all, Dad had left her his entire estate, much of which came from community property when my parents were married and from money inherited from our grandparents and great grandparents – all real estate, art, stocks and bonds, furnishings and cash.

Instead of giving us a chance to talk this over, she was incensed, immediately on the offensive. "Here you are waiting until your father is dead and now you are claiming something that happened in the late '50s. Why do you wait so long to claim these paintings? You brought up painting when you sued your father and there were no documents then." I explained that since Rusty had just notified us, we only now had the documents showing proper ownership and that unless we could come to an agreement with her, legally, for time reasons, we had to act quickly.

"It's too late," she said. "Your time is past. Anyway, painting is mine. And anyone or their children who makes my life difficult is out of will. Besides, Rusty is using you as a tool. I am going to send him to jail." Later I heard from my sister that she was told that if she filed a claim with Hap and me, she, too, would be out of Denise's will.

Having spent from 1986 to 1992 in legal battles with my family, I was extremely reluctant to reenter the fray. I knew that Denise was vindictive and irrational, possibly even more so than my father had been and that she, too, would spare no expense to win. Should we prevail and regain possession of the painting, it wouldn't be without great cost. But a deeper voice urged me once again to speak up.

Again there were some incentives: The painting was the vehicle that brought the four siblings back together and fighting Denise for it would end any possibility of any of us having a future relationship with her. Hilary, Hap and I decided to file our claim, separate from the one Rusty had already filed and once again we were embroiled in a legal battle. This time, however, we were on the same side. For the first time in many years, I felt hopeful about the possibility of our family getting back together again.

As expected, Denise responded with fury, using my father's name and the press as weapons to promote her cause. An expert in building up her image to her advantage, she made sure that articles portraying her as the grieving widow and us as disrespectful stepchildren appeared in newspapers and magazines across the country. We were "the four ingrates," greedy, ungrateful, money-grubbing children, who had "no compunctions about attacking their dead father's name."

She aired her own version of the family's dirty laundry, exaggerating the amount of money we had and claiming we were accusing our father of "stealing" money from us. In her words, we were trying to "extract more money.... How can these four ingrates stoop so low as to claim their father hoodwinked them?" She accused us of trashing his reputation, especially despicable because he was not here to defend himself. She made herself out to be the protector of his good name from his ungrateful and greedy children.

These were accusations coming from a woman who had inherited my father's entire estate. In addition to other valuable paintings, such as the beautiful Degas that my father had given my mother for her birthday, she also had in her possession all of my grandmother's and mother's silver, my grandmother's copper and her vast Persian rug collection, my mother's Flora Danica china and the engraved silver plate and exquisite silver bowl that the San Francisco firemen gave to my grandmother for her work after the 1906 earthquake. She even hung the record-setting kudu horns that I shot in Mozambique in 1963 up at the ranch. (They were featured in the October 14, 2003 issue of *HELLO!*). And she was now furious that she couldn't also have the one painting that clearly had always belonged to the four children. Calling us greedy and ungrateful, she projected onto us the very qualities that accurately described her.

During the flurry of unflattering articles that made Denise look petty and transparent, we remained silent, hoping that Denise might come to her senses and realize with no legal leg to stand on, she should return the painting to us, the rightful owners. Of course she refused to do this or to consider compensating us at all for the Sisley painting, sold in 1978, which we had also owned.

During one of our pretrial depositions with Denise, she repeatedly tried to give the impression that she knew nothing about the ownership of the Morisot painting other than that it belonged to my father and he gave it to her. She claimed to have heard only one discussion regarding the painting, years ago, up at the ranch when my father and Rusty were talking about it.

How then, I wondered, could she explain away her comments to me during our recent telephone conversation when I told her we must file a claim before the statute of limitations runs out? And how could she forget a crudely drafted document we found during discovery, entitled "Feeding the Swans," oil on canvas, 22" x 29", by Berthe Morisot and dated July 13, 1993 (written soon after my father's stroke and signed in his trembling hand) that she also signed to "prove" her ownership? And why did this document specify only this one painting from my parents' collection unless she was worried about its ownership?

By this time we knew that Denise had a tendency to contradict herself. In that article in *W* she was quoted as saying, "I'm very outspoken, but at least you know where you stand with me. I'm never going to say I'm your friend and stab you in the back. If I'm your friend, I'm your friend." A few years later, she elaborated, in the October 2003 issue of

HELLO! magazine, where she was quoted as saying, "... they know that one thing I never do is gossip about people behind their backs."

But people who run in her circle tell a different story. "She has names for her 'friends' like 'The Climber,' 'The Town Drunk,' 'The Little Shop Girl,' and 'The Nurse.' And she only keeps her 'friends' as long as they serve her purposes, dropping them quickly when they are no longer useful to her. When Frank Jordan was mayor of San Francisco, Denise included him and his wife, Wendy, in many of her parties, but when Willie Brown was elected the new mayor, she was in full view at his victory party, soon thereafter dropping the Jordans from her party list. "That's understandable," said an acquaintance. "Willie's the winner; he's now the one with power."

A former friend of hers, L., told me the following story of the transparency of Denise's loyalty. During L.'s painful and acrimonious divorce, her husband's lawyer said something in one of the numerous hearings that he wouldn't ordinarily know. L. wondered how he had obtained this information, suddenly realizing the only way he could have was through her "good" friend Denise. To confirm her suspicions, L. told Denise that she desperately wanted a certain asset from the marriage (she didn't; she wanted something else instead). Sure enough in their next legal confrontation, L.'s husband told her he'd never give her this certain asset and countered with a different offer. Using Denise's treachery to her advantage, L. now had a pipeline to her ex that eventually landed her exactly the settlement she wanted.

Aside from her claims to being a wonderful friend, Denise also paints a grand picture of her upbringing in Belgrade.

Raised in a prominent family, whose wealth, she claims, was taken by the Nazis and then the Communists, she likes to tell of her escape from Yugoslavia and her rescue by a charming sea captain. On several occasions she has also alluded to an early marriage to a rich, older Italian man before she ended up in Hollywood, married to famous director Vincente Minnelli.

There seemed to be a disconnection between what she said and how she acted. At her elegant retreat at the ranch, a family member told me she writes signs on shirt cardboards and tapes them in strategic places throughout the house. "Turn lights out." "Close door." When I read in a recent *San Francisco Chronicle* article that she mentioned "good-looking toilet brushes and dust pans as reasons why she shops at a local discount store, I wondered about her upper-class upbringing.

Denise has demonstrated other behavior that poses questions for me. My husband and I saw her at a friend's black-tie anniversary party while we were in the middle of our lawsuit over the Berthe Morisot painting. Approaching Denise, my husband jokingly said, "Denise, I bet you ten dollars we win the painting." She turned to him and said, "Why don't you go [expletive] yourself?" in a voice loud enough so her seatmate, a prominent New York gallery owner and also a friend of ours, flinched.

Her aggressively acquisitive nature belied her patrician claims as well. After Dad died, Rusty filed three lawsuits against Denise. In the biggest suit Rusty stated that his father promised him the ranch and 65 percent of the assets from his father's estate. As evidence Rusty presented a two-page, typed letter on Dad's stationery, dated June 1, 1994, and signed by father and son. In the last paragraph Dad stated he had left a letter in which "I have also requested that the HE ranch be left to you if you agree to keep it for 15 years and I have also requested that you be given 65 percent of the residue of my estate."

Rusty told me that when Mr. Chodos, his lawyer, in one of the many depositions, asked Denise how she could explain that Prentis left her 100% of his estate, she said it was because he loved her 100%. "If you love someone 100%, can't you still give some of the money to the children?" he asked. "No, he loved me 100%," she insisted. Even though Dad's request was in several letters to his wife, Denise denied it was her husband's intent. (The judge agreed with Denise.)

Rusty had his own legal battle going on with Denise separately from Hilary, Hap and me. One day his lawyer, Hillel Chodos, called to ask if he and my brother could meet with me. I was somewhat surprised since I hadn't had any relationship with Rusty in over sixteen years. But I was also curious and so I agreed to the meeting.

When they walked into our house, my old love for him beckoned me right back to his side. Even though I was sad and angry about how he had treated me his entire adult life, I once again felt like my brother's "little" sister, the girl who saw inside this distant, tall, handsome man to his sweet, gentle core. I was the girl who would do anything to help him.

Hillel got right to the point. He asked me to testify on my brother's behalf in his separate lawsuit against Denise. Even though I had anticipated their request, I was surprised at my brother's lack of conscience. I had never had an apology from him. Did he feel no remorse over how he'd treated me for the last fifteen years? I glanced over at my brother, but he didn't look back at me, perhaps a sign that he didn't feel great about the way he'd behaved. "Rusty," I said, "I love you, but unless you can be accountable for how much you've hurt me, I'm reluctant to testify for you, however much I want you to prevail over Denise."

Before Rusty could respond, Hillel stood up and asked me to join him in the hall. He told me what a difficult time my brother'd had with our father and assured me that Rusty did in fact feel bad about all that had happened. Even though I was disappointed my brother couldn't tell me this himself, I felt sorry for him. After all, I said to myself, maybe if I helped him this time, he would open up to me and we could rebuild our relationship. Besides, however hard it was for me, it was another opportunity for me to speak up against misuses of power and stand up for my mother and our family. I decided to say yes. So before I had settled my own suit with Denise, I found myself in front of a judge, testifying for my brother.

When I walked into the courthouse, I saw large, blown-up portions of my father's will along one side of the room. Even from a distance I could read where he had specifically disinherited my children and me. Sitting to the left, Denise was flanked by lawyers along with other people whom I didn't know. Even though Denise had no compunctions about calling me greedy and ungrateful, I was nervous having to describe my own experience of her cruelty, something I knew would infuriate her. I had been called in specifically to validate the claim that Denise was vindictive and less than objective about her stepchildren.

I walked to the stand, where I was sworn in and answered Hillel's introductory questions. Then he asked, "Has

Denise ever treated you unfairly in any way?" "Yes," I said and then I told my story about Denise's not allowing me to see my father when he was dying. I said that I was forever grateful to a friend who knew how sad I was that I couldn't reach my father. When I mentioned by name that kind friend who brought my note to my father and told me he was happy to receive it, I saw Denise sit up straighter in her chair. Only then did I realize that she had not known who had given the note to Dad for me. I added that I never did have a chance to say good-bye to my father. I was aware that there was no other sound in the courtroom as I spoke.

Later when our lawyer deposed Denise, she mentioned that this friend had brought me up to see Dad and that I was able to spend some time with him while he was still conscious. Of course that hadn't happened. I had never been allowed to see my father until he was near death in a coma. She added that my father was furious I was there, also claiming that after I left his bedside at the hospital, he told her "I never want to see Linda again, even when I am dying." Somehow I knew then that the truth of my testimony for my brother had struck a home run. Denise soon settled out of court with Hilary, Hap and me.

Rusty was also victorious on two different counts and so I realized the judge believed me. Rusty called me from his car phone to say a short thank you and that was that. But for a long time I saved a message his lawyer, Hillel Chodos, left on our answering machine. "I am calling you to thank you personally for coming to testify at the trial. I really appreciate it. I know it was not an easy undertaking for you. I can tell you the judge was absolutely riveted by your testimony. She ascribed great significance to it, as did everybody else in the courtroom. I think it was extremely helpful to the extent that Rusty prevailed and this success, it's attributable, albeit a little indirectly, largely to your testimony." I was so grateful for his acknowledgement and kind words.

Denise and my brother still had another legal matter to decide – the verification of who owned the remaining quarter of the painting. The court date was set. Once again Mr. Chodos asked if I would testify on my brother's behalf and once again I said yes. Arriving at Superior Court, I didn't expect to see many people there, generally the rule when it came to cases like this, but when I looked at Denise, I saw sitting behind her many people whom I later learned were from Glide Memorial Church, a life-inspiring sanctuary that helps anyone in need. Those appearing to support her looked like a cross-section of working class San Franciscans and not those who dined at Stars or regularly attended her society events. Somehow she had convinced these hard working people to come to court. Then I understood: Denise wanted the jury to see her as a woman of the people, not as the greedy socialite she actually was.

Remembering my previous time in court, I felt nervous all over again and wondered if I would be able to hold my own. This time I faced Patrick Hallinan, a well-connected, good-old-boy lawyer whose brother, Terrence, was the district attorney of San Francisco. Aggressive and sarcastic, he made sure the jury was well aware of his disdain for me, this ungrateful witness. However, his intimidating tactics and rapid-fire questions, rather than throwing me off balance, only made me concentrate more. I was once again on the tennis court, focused on doing my best and hopefully winning. At the break I was standing at the water fountain when

Mr. Hallinan approached me. "You're a great witness," he said.

When Denise was on the stand, she played the grieving widow part well, so well in fact that Rusty's lawyer referred to her display of apparent emotion as a "death scene from *Camille*, a wilting-violet act." However, she made the mistake of saying that my father had given her the painting as a birthday gift, directly contradicting what she had said in earlier depositions about only overhearing the painting mentioned once up at the ranch in a conversation between my father and Rusty. In the closing arguments, Hallinan accused my brother of being a "Judas," a son who turned on his generous father.

The Superior Court jurors thought otherwise. Clearly, even with her Glide Memorial supporters by her side, Denise's story was so unbelievable that the foreperson came back shortly after starting deliberations to ask about guidelines for punitive damages. Unfortunately, they were not allowed. In a unanimous decision, deliberating for less than three hours, the jurors found that Denise Hale had no right to the painting, ending for the moment, a legal battle that never should have happened in the first place.

Later, Steve Nash, a director from the museum where the painting was being held, called me. Although Denise had signed away the painting, he told me she wanted the frame back. "You're not serious," I asked, not believing his words. He assured me he was. "Under no condition," I said. Edward Lempinen, a *Chronicle* reporter, interviewed me for his February 14, 1998, article. In it he wrote, "According to Bucklin, Denise Hale approached museum officials recently and told them that although she had signed away the painting, she wanted the frame back.... Steven Nash, associate director of the city's fine arts museums, declined to comment on that report."

In another *Chronicle* article, Denise lashed out a few last times. "I wanted them (the Hale children) out of my hair a long time ago...." Interesting, I thought to myself, that she would state this publicly now, confirming what had been so obviously a goal of hers from the very start. In a Page Six article in the *New York Post* she described herself as a "Serbian woman" with a "long memory," but indicated that there's one place she wouldn't remember her husband's children and that was in her will.

In the February 1998 issue of *W*, Denise had some reactions to the litigation. When I read her words, I could feel Denise speaking to me and my siblings: "Don't waste your energy fighting your enemies. Just go to end of river and wait for body of your enemy to pass by." In regard to her travails and again in reference to her four stepchildren, she said, "This is how I see myself: as a piece of meat. There are hyenas everywhere, circling. But one hyena says to the other, 'Watch out, this Serbian meat is tough. I just broke all my teeth on it.'"

Something else she said in the *W* article on how she dealt with my mother's death took my breath away with its callousness. "How I dealt with (the scandal) was very simple. I have two things I live my life by. The first is: People are not my problem. I am problem to the people. What they think is not my concern. My other thing is: Live and let live." In all but her last comment, I thought Denise described herself perfectly.

With Denise by my father's side, his demons tumbled

forth unchecked, matching hers and he inflicted great pain on those who loved him most. When I read in the newspapers about my father changing his will at whim dozens of times, bequeathing $200,000 to his two German shepherds while disowning his own children and grandchildren, I wondered whatever happened to that family man who lectured us incessantly on the importance of family. Why couldn't he see how cruel and mercurial his power world could be and how transient its rewards?

The losses we suffered at the hands of Denise were considerable, but the one I felt most poignantly was that of the ranch. When Denise invited us to the memorial service she had planned there for Dad, I hesitated before finally deciding to go. I realized how important it was for me to return and show my children the place that was most dear to me, the place where I had been the happiest. My husband drove and I sat next to him. In the back were Christian, John and Nick. As we crossed the final cattle guard, my heart quickened. Around the bend and over the arroyo that was filled with bay and buckeye trees, we came to the corrals and rundown stable. Off to our right shimmered Sulphur Creek, the river of my youth.

I asked Bill to stop and we all piled out of the car. I had an irrepressible need to sit by the edge of the river. We walked across the gravel bar; the boys wandered off and immediately started a rock-skipping contest. But I knelt down and scooped up handfuls of coarse, warm riverbed. Putting my feet in the sun-warmed water, I closed my eyes and breathed in the pungent smell of skunk cabbage and felt the sun hot on my back. I sat there for a long time, gathering the river in my arms, saying my farewells.

Then we drove beside the now deserted corrals of Barney, Flicka, Diablo and Dune, passing the huge live oak tree that had shaded Jim's tiny cabin and our first home and until the big house, my parents' love house. Until my mother died, it was the house that had burst to the seams with our friends and our parents' friends, with the girls' dorm and the boys' dorm, the games of charades and moonlit swims, croquet, ping pong, tennis, dominoes and lively lunches and dinners with 20 or more, all ages, squeezing in at the long, wooden dining table.

We parked and walked towards the house. Christian, John and Nick were silent, momentarily stilled by the somberness of the occasion. They were cognizant of how much I loved the ranch and while they never knew my father, they were also aware of the despair his recent death caused me.

A cool blast of air hit us as we entered the living room. I adjusted my eyes to the darkness and took a deep breath, steeling myself for the upcoming encounter with Denise, Carmella Scaggs and her support group of friends. Word had spread rapidly in San Francisco; already Hilary, Rusty, Hap and I had heard, hours after Dad died, that Denise was inheriting everything.

Although it had been almost 20 years since I'd been back to the ranch, I remembered every detail of the panoramic view from the back porch. But when I went outside, I gasped. Now thick shrubs and trees enclosed the lawn and the swimming pool, completely obscuring any hint of the wilderness beyond. I felt claustrophobic, hemmed in and in a strange way detached, because this was no longer the ranch as I knew it. There was no hint that a wild, beautiful vista lay just beyond the impenetrable trees that surrounded the house.

As I stood off by myself on the back porch, memories tumbled through me. I became a young girl again, part of a family that gathered here as twilight descended and my mother and I, shoulders touching, sitting together on the creaky wicker lounge. In my memory, we looked out over the hills that were bathed in the soft, evening light and for miles saw no sign anywhere of human inhabitants, only oak trees, steep drops down to the river, dark boulders and rugged land dipping and curving towards the horizon.

The sun went down behind the far-off coastal mountain range, leaving behind a wide crimson slash that stretched across the west. Stars slowly started to dot the indigo blue night sky. I wished I may, I wished I might, have this wish I wished tonight. I wished to be right here next to my mother forever.

Crickets hummed, bats swooped and swerved close to our heads and I heard the faint howl of a coyote. Darkness surrounded us. Still in my memory, I looked eastward and held my breath, watching, waiting for the full moon to rise up over the distant mountains, whose rocky edges seemed drawn on the horizon with a fine silver pencil. Suddenly it burst forth, sailing free and clear, a perfect orb that caressed the landscape with its borrowed light.

All these images raced through my mind as I stood on the porch looking at what could be a country garden anywhere. I was struck by the way this change from simple and wild to manicured and obviously moneyed so illustrated the life my father chose to live with Denise in contrast to the life he lived before her. I wondered if he regretted his choices. If he could unring the bell and come back from death, would he turn back to us, his family and gather us together out on the porch and point out a wisp of steam from the distant geysers? Would he cherish us, celebrate us, urge us on to consider possibilities beyond our reckoning? Would he hold my mother close and whisper sweet nothings in her ear? Would he find the Big Dipper and the North Star and assure us that forever, as long as we could look out over these hills and see the stars, we wouldn't get lost?

I turned and followed the others over to a large oak tree and listened, as a Serbian priest mumbled incomprehensible sounds over my father's ashes. Later she asked me if I wanted to ride in the jeep to show the boys the ranch that I knew Dad had given away to her. I accepted, somehow sensing that this might be my farewell to the place I so loved.

As we rounded a curve higher up on the ranch, suddenly the same view I remembered hit me full in the face. "Whoa," John exclaimed, "this makes me feel like flying." I realized then that everything and nothing stayed the same. I realized, too, that I could and couldn't hold on to what I'd lost, but that no matter what, I could find my way.

12

Finding My Way

Sometimes I found myself looking back to the hopeful woman I had once been, the one who believed in my family and never thought they would turn away from me. Over the years of fighting with my family, I experienced many emotions – at first hope, then despair, anger and finally determination, all bumping up against the love I always felt for them.

It took me many years and countless disappointments, but my illusions were now firmly dispelled. In the harsh light of all that happened, I saw a father who never heard me, an older brother who heard me but who left my side and a sister and younger brother who didn't want to hear me. After our lawsuit with Denise, we were at least talking to each other, but I didn't hold out much hope we could reconnect on any deeper level.

Then a year after the lawsuits ended, my sister made the first move, inviting us to a Christmas dinner. Despite my misgivings, my husband and I, plus Christian, Kris, John and Nick, decided to go. I think this was the first time all of us – the four Hale children plus spouses and our children – were together. As I looked around the table, I was flooded with happy memories of dinners we'd had when we were young and still a family. And then Hap cracked a joke, bringing me back to this bittersweet reunion. We all laughed, momentarily joined. At that moment, the walls that had grown up around my heart to protect me from my family began to crack.

In the months that followed, both Hilary and Hap contacted me to apologize for the hurt they'd caused me. "Linda, I'm just not like you," my sister said. "You always question things. You like to explore below the surface. I don't go there. I don't like to cause trouble. But I'm sorry I wasn't there to support you."

And then Hap called and seemed genuinely happy to talk with me. "Hap," I said, "why are you being so nice to me?" He paused. "You deserve it. After how mean I have been to you for so long, now it's time for me to make amends."

Hilary, Hap and I took small steps towards each other, trying to mend the torn patches in the fabric of our family. I reconnected with Anne, Hap's wife, and delighted in them and the fun-loving, wonderful life they've created together in their beautiful home high in the redwoods just south of San Francisco. We had a few dinners together. I even hosted a luncheon for Hilary's 60th birthday.

And she and I planned a baby shower for my son Christian and his wife Kris. Listening to *Madame Butterfly* as I arranged flowers for the party, I thought of my mother. I thought, too, of Ditzy, her best friend, who'd just died. I could picture them both, now perched together on a star. In my mind, they have their arms around each other's waists, my mother's hair is loose, a red halo framing her face and Ditzy wears a colorful scarf. They are laughing and leaning forward to get a better look at our party preparations.

At my mother's death, she was about to become a grandmother, just as I now was. How I wished she could be at our house with Hilary and me. She would be eagerly waiting to embrace Hap and Anne. How she would smile, her face alight, when Christian and Kris, pregnant with her great grandchild, arrived, their sweetness surrounding them. She would watch for Rusty, too, even though the rest of us doubted he'd make it. (He didn't.)

What a thrill my mother would have gotten out of how well her grandchildren were doing. I wished she could have seen my sister and me as mothers ourselves and shared in all the joys and trials that every parent experiences. How she would have enjoyed getting to know our children.

I could picture her talking with Christian about different wines, perhaps tasting a special one he recommends, or seeing him be the wonderful husband and father he is. How she would have loved hearing John play classical music on the piano, as she had done, or admired a beautiful painting he'd painted. What fun she would have had watching Nick lead his varsity lacrosse team to victory or stand up as a voice for his peers, a great friend, as she was, to so many.

Rusty, still the wild card, remains distant, roaming elusively around the periphery of our family. I tried to keep in touch with him, but he has made little effort to stay connected. Mostly I learn about him through friends. "Oh, I just had dinner with your brother. He's in great shape. He played the guitar and sang for us," one of his friends told me. When I heard these words, a little piece of my heart broke off. I remembered that solid, loving older brother I once knew and had difficulty matching him to the brother I no longer know. Never did I imagine that our lives would separate as they did, that we would become adversaries and finally strangers.

One of the last times I saw Rusty was when a close family friend died. I went over to him after the service and hugged him, but he quickly turned towards the person on his left. Later at the reception I tried again to engage him, but he brushed me off. When I told a friend what had happened, I couldn't stop crying. "Linda," he said, "you've got to let go. Just let go."

"How can I let go of my heart?" I asked him.

"You must let go of the end result," he answered. Suddenly I understood. I couldn't make this brother love me, so I had to let go of hoping that he ever would. But I love him still and wish him well on his journey through this life.

Although I wish my mother could see us now, I'm also grateful she never knew what happened to our family. How could she have withstood the pain of seeing her four children fight for so long? Or lived knowing her most beloved son might have stopped being her champion? Would her heart have broken all over again, knowing that he, like my father, seemed to have lost his way?

Evenings at the ranch, my mother would always wish upon the first star. Once she leaned into me and whispered, "Linda, I always make the same wish – for you kids to be happy." Now that I have children, I understand and I, too, repeat that wish.

Throughout my family struggles, disillusioned and heartbroken, I never stopped believing in the power and goodness of family. Rather, the disintegration of my family of origin made me cherish my own family all the more and strengthened my resolve to be as good a parent as I could.

I no longer believe my father's words about our 'perfect' family, knowing now that there is no such thing as this. Accepting the imperfections of the family I have created helps me be less hard on myself when I have failed in some way. Finally I understand that I can't make everyone love and connect with each other. I can only do the best I can do.

I've made many mistakes, but what makes me happy is my knowing that I haven't repeated my mother's elusive loving or my father's terrorizing, silencing behavior. Instead, I've raised three sons who aren't afraid to speak, as I was for so long and who are courageous enough to trust the individual paths they choose.

Looking at my failed relationships, both within my family and with 'friends', I realized I wanted to communicate to others the many positive things I had learned and to make amends. I wrote a letter to my ex-husband apologizing for my hurtful behavior and thanking him for being the wonderful man he is.

With a close friend I coauthored a book on women's friendships, *Come Rain or Come Shine*, now in its second printing, that helped me understand how to be a better person and friend. I wrote about the importance of being as conscious as I could in my relationships and about the power of love.

Then I wrote this book, another step in my journey to express my voice. A few months back I sent a copy to my sister and my younger brother. My sister called me. "Linda,

I just finished your manuscript. Your heart and soul are so deep. It is so powerful; I could picture everything. I cried all the way through it. I have no problem with it; it's totally fair."

And then my younger brother calls me. "I like it a lot. You are very accurate in describing what happened. I have no problems whatsoever with what you say." I felt so grateful both for their acknowledgment of what had happened to us and their support of me. Finally, they heard and understood my voice.

With my newfound strength and some sense of clarity about my family, I decided I was ready to try to figure out what might have happened the night my mother died. I tracked down what police investigation records remained in the City and County of San Francisco Department of Records.

Steeling myself, I went down to City Hall and combed through the files. In reading the Coroner's Register #640, I was immediately struck by an inconsistency. "There was a spent bullet, lying at deceased's feet and there was a .38 caliber revolver, which contained 5 live cartridges and 1 spent cartridge under the hammer. This gun was lying in an open top drawer of a built-in series of drawers in front of deceased's body." How, I wondered, did the gun end up back in the top drawer of Dad's dresser?

I speculated. Perhaps in a completely irrational moment, my father picked it up from my mother's side and put it back in the drawer. But it was hard for me to believe my father would implicate himself in this way. He was very smart and his affair with Denise had been too public. Tight with money, he understood that under California community property law, a divorce after 33 years of marriage would have cost him millions of dollars and perhaps the ranch. He would have fought his hardest to give up as few of his assets as possible.

I continued to read. No suicide note was found. Yet the premises were neither sealed nor searched, which was unusual when Homicide was called in. Inspector Kracke, the homicide investigator who was on the scene soon after my mother had died, ordered no powder or paraffin tests, simple procedures that could have cleared up any doubts as to the nature of her death. At the end of the record I found the hauntingly final words: "Gunshot – apparent suicide." As far as the authorities were concerned, Case #640 was closed.

Not included in this report was the only thing I knew for sure about the last hour of my mother's life. She had been in bed reading and then she got up. I remembered back to the night she died, when I sat on the side of her bed and let my fingers touch the bedcovers where she last lay alive. I noticed she'd put a bookmark in her book to mark her place, unusual, I thought at the time, for someone planning suicide. I had no answers.

After my father died in February 1996, a friend gave me an article from *Quest* magazine entitled "North by Northeast," by David Patrick Columbia, about a phone call between two lovers and how the woman heard the gunshot that killed her lover's wife. When I read it, I started to shake. Chills ran up my spine. Clearly, at least to me, Columbia's story of the people he called "X" and "Y" was about Denise and my parents. I was stunned by his details of the night my mother died.

As he told it, X (Denise) and Y (my father) had been talking on the phone and Mrs. Y (my mother), in another part of the mansion, was eavesdropping. She interrupted, saying "Harry," (not his real name), "if you don't get off the phone with that ... right this minute, I'm going to shoot myself." To which "Harry" replies, "Be my guest." Then X and Y heard the report of a gun going off followed by the thud of the body.

I called the magazine Mr. Columbia works for in New York and located him. When I got him on the phone, I introduced myself as Y's daughter. There was a brief silence; then I told him why I was calling. "I understand why you waited 27 years until my father's death to write this, but how did you ever come up with this story?" I asked. His article provided the only outside details I had ever heard about what might have happened that night to explain my mother's death.

He explained. That very night, one of his closest friends M., a prominent Hollywood personality, told him this story. Just as M. was leaving to meet Columbia for a late dinner, the phone rang and M. answered. It was Denise, urgently asking to speak to M.'s houseguest. (Columbia told me the names, but I promised not to reveal them.) M. heard his houseguest, a close female friend, exclaiming, "Oh no, oh dear, how horrible, oh I can't believe it." When she hung up, M. asked her what happened. At first she said she was sworn to secrecy, but with a little encouragement, she told him. Soon everyone from coast to coast was talking about this terrible night.

After my conversation with Columbia, my thoughts swirled. If my mother were eavesdropping, as Columbia's account suggested, she would have been in her bedroom where the phone was. But my mother's body was found in my father's study, a far distance away from the telephone. Would Denise and my father have been able to hear the report of the shot and the sound of my mother's body falling?

Most of all, it was those three cruel words—"be my guest"—words my father supposedly said to my mother right before her death, that banged against my throat. Many times when my father had been angry with me, he would use those very words—a dare of sorts—to show his disdain and push me to an uncertain place emotionally, where suddenly I would be at his mercy. I was blown away by the possibility that Columbia's account might be true and that my father, in fact, might have been callous enough to dare my mother to end her life.

Despite the shock of these revelations, I was gradually able to come to some sense of peace with all that had happened. It was on a summer day in Montana several years after my father's death, when everything seemed to come together for me. That day, I hiked to the top of a ridge in Montana and looked out over miles of uninhabited land, with sage brush and potholes where ducks hid, dotting the landscape. I wished my father were by my side, so I could show him the pair of sand hill cranes and point out the dramatic Blackfoot Mountains to the south. As I stood watching thunderheads build up beyond the Bob Marshall wilderness, gathering force for an afternoon storm, I remembered back to when I finally found the courage to stand up to him.

It had been a long journey extracting myself from my father's dominance and my own self-destructive avoidance of confronting him to my self-assertion. Finally I was able to acknowledge his gifts to me, sensing how his exacting standards and sense of discipline had grounded me and urged me forward. His intellectual curiosity and love for debate had challenged me and his risk-taking ways, especially in the physical realm, had helped me to be courageous. Ironically, he had given me part of his toughness, the very trait I had needed in my battles with him. And his repressiveness had ignited me, ultimately making me determined to express myself.

I also realized he had offered me many opportunities to experience beauty, imparting to me his love of art, opera and fine wine. I grew up in lovely surroundings that his keen eye for beauty masterminded. Most of all he had exposed me to the wonder and magic of nature, for he loved best, as I did too, all places wild. Whenever I sit watching mallard and widgeon land on Gundog Lake, the Buttes framed in crimson beyond, I think of him. Whenever I walk the banks of the North Fork, casting my fly into waters where I hope hungry trout lie, I remember myself as a girl, sitting quietly next to him at Fraser Creek, waiting for him to hand me his rod after he'd hooked a fish.

I am certain he felt betrayed by the daughter who was once his favorite child; I know I hurt him terribly. I'm sure he never understood why. As I continued on my hike, tears streamed down my cheeks. Suddenly, words I had been unable to say to him, because I was too afraid his power would overwhelm my love, tumbled forth. "I'm sorry I hurt you," I said. "I had to challenge you so I could live. I only wanted you to see me; I never stopped loving you." Even though my father had been dead for two years, I was strangely comforted by what I said, these words he never heard, forgiving myself for not being courageous enough to tell him this in life.

Off in the distance, a hawk cried and one answered back. These sounds conjured up a picture I had in my memory of my father when he was about 59, close to my age as I write this. He was sitting at the edge of our porch at the ranch and Sebastian, his old black lab, was lying at his feet. An opera played in the background. The sun was setting, the hills nearby whitewashed with the evening light. When I reached his side, he turned towards me and I noticed he had been crying. Whether he was moved by the beauty of the music or the land around him or whether he cried for a deeper reason, I would never know.

Here, as I stood on the rim of a hill in Montana, I saw him – finally – for what he was. This strong, willful father really was not the powerful man I thought he was; beneath his ironclad exterior resided an insecure, scared soul, a man so afraid of being vulnerable and kind that he used force instead on those who loved him. He was simply a man who struggled through his life as we all do, trying to find his way, sometimes succeeding, many times stumbling and I forgave him as I had just forgiven myself.

It was almost dark when I walked back to camp. Above my head the night jars swooped through the twilight sky, catching mosquitoes. A bat flicked by. In the distance I heard my dear husband of 29 years, my three sons and daughter-in-law laughing and talking. When I rounded the bend, there they were, seated around the campfire. Christian looked up and waved and my heart settled down to a steady beat.

Later that night, I lay on my cot looking up at a black Montana sky, the big splash of the Milky Way overhead. A satellite hurtled by. Off to my left I saw a shooting star and to my right the Pleiades clustered brightly.

I thought of my complicated parents, of Frances, of my beloved brothers and sister, of my need to go deep and follow that path of introspection I could never run from. My parents lost their way, but in so doing, they helped me find mine.

And I thought of my mother, my mother, who follows me everywhere. When the spring rain touches my cheek, I feel her caress. When my son slips his hand in mine, I remember reaching out for hers and when the wind rustles the leaves of a black oak tree, I hear her sigh. My sweet, kind mother – her gentle soul wraps its arms around me.

In this life's journey I finally realized how important it is to continue to claim my own voice. As I recovered my emotional balance over the years, I looked deep within me, reaching out towards the girl whom my nurse Frances and my mother had loved. I remembered how sturdy and beloved I felt and how happy I was when I said what I wanted to say. I began to understand how staying a silent victim like my mother damaged my soul and how speaking up truthfully empowered it. My mother's death changed everything for me. I would never again be willing to settle for silence.

I stopped blaming myself for not speaking up for her and for not being lovable enough to prevent her death. I realized that her final actions were directed towards my father, not towards anything I did or didn't do. She was in too much pain and my father overpowered her. Now, I, her daughter, could carry her torch of love and realize that she did indeed love us as much as she could.

I was also able to accept that my mother's death did not diminish the vitality and excellence of the life she lived. To honor her memory, I raised the funds needed to have the new library at Grace Cathedral named the Marialice King Hale Library. Some days when I am there, I imagine she is looking over my shoulder. I can almost feel her fingers covering mine, helping me turn the pages of this book. I believe that my mother knows – finally – that she was beloved and her life was worthwhile.

For my happiness I need to face the truth about myself and what happened in our family; knowing my true story helps me live and be alive. As a family, we had some wonderful times as well as some devastating ones. Being able to hold both truths helps me navigate the waters of my life, pulling me steadily towards a place of greater clarity and with it the space for more love and forgiveness.

That night in Montana, I turned my head again towards the black, starry sky. Spotting the Big Dipper, I traced the two bottom stars up to the North Star. Now I was no longer lost. Suddenly, I felt God was all around me and within me and I knew that wherever I went, God would help me find my way.

I am filled with love.
Hold my hand; hold my hand.
I am beloved. We are all beloved.

Additional copies of this book may be obtained
from your bookstore
or by contacting
Hope Publishing House
P.O. Box 60008
Pasadena, CA 91116 - U.S.A.
(626) 792-6123 / (800) 326-2671
Fax (626) 792-2121
E-mail: hopepub@sbcglobal.net
www.hope-pub.com